Library of
Davidson College

PROBABILITY AND
HUME'S INDUCTIVE
SCEPTICISM

PROBABILITY AND HUME'S INDUCTIVE SCEPTICISM

D. C. STOVE

OXFORD
AT THE CLARENDON PRESS
1973

Oxford University Press, Ely House, London W.1
GLASGOW NEW YORK TORONTO MELBOURNE WELLINGTON
CAPE TOWN IBADAN NAIROBI DAR ES SALAAM LUSAKA ADDIS ABABA
DELHI BOMBAY CALCUTTA MADRAS KARACHI LAHORE DACCA
KUALA LUMPUR SINGAPORE HONG KONG TOKYO

© Oxford University Press 1973

*Printed in Great Britain
at the University Press, Oxford
by Vivian Ridler
Printer to the University*

TO MY WIFE JESS
AND OUR CHILDREN
ROBERT AND JUDITH

ACKNOWLEDGEMENTS

I have profited greatly from discussing probability and induction with Mr. Manfred von Thun during the years 1967-70, when he was first an undergraduate and then a graduate student of the University of Sydney. Much more than that, however; the materials of Chapter 5 sections (*iii*) and (*iv*) of the present work are entirely due to Mr. von Thun. Just how important those sections are for my argument as a whole will be evident to any reader. In fact, along with Chapters 2-4, they make up the heart of the book.

All of the other pieces which make up the book were clear in my mind before Mr. von Thun supplied me with the argument given in Chapter 5 section (*iii*). None of them, consequently, needed to be altered after he had done so. But his argument has helped me a second time, since it was easily adaptable so as to become an addition to my other arguments in Chapter 6.

For critical comments on the penultimate draft of the book, I am especially indebted to Mr. J. L. Mackie and (again) to Mr. von Thun. But Professor J. J. C. Smart and Professor D. M. Armstrong also helped me by their comments on that draft; for which I thank them.

D.C.S.

University of Sydney
1971

CONTENTS

INTRODUCTION. Object and plan of the book — 1

PART ONE. SOME REMARKS ON PROBABILITY
1. Chiefly on Statements of Logical Probability — 5

PART TWO. HUME'S ARGUMENT FOR INDUCTIVE SCEPTICISM: IDENTIFICATION
2. Its Structure and Content — 27
3. Its Suppressed Premisses — 46
4. Its Further Interpretation and Generalization — 53

PART THREE. HUME'S ARGUMENT FOR INDUCTIVE SCEPTICISM: EVALUATION
5. The Falsity of its Sceptical Conclusion — 65
6. The Falsity of its Deductivist Premiss — 74
7. The Truth and Importance of its Fallibilist Consequence — 90
8. Our Historical Debts to Hume's Argument for Scepticism — 98
9. Concluding Remarks — 111

APPENDIX — 117

INDEX — 133

INTRODUCTION: OBJECT AND PLAN OF THE BOOK

For the sceptical view which he took of inductive inference, David Hume only ever gave one argument. That argument is the sole subject-matter of this book. My object is first to identify this argument, and then to evaluate it. The latter is what is attempted in Part Three (Chapters 5-9) of the book.

The main results of my evaluation can be summarized as follows. The sceptical conclusion of Hume's argument (I claim in Chapter 5 to show) is false. It rests (I claim in Chapter 6 to show) on a certain identifiable premiss which is false. Not all of my conclusions, however, are hostile to Hume's argument. Its true premisses (I claim in Chapter 7 to show) suffice to prove an important negative conclusion, though not a sceptical one, about inductive inferences. And what has historically been learnt from Hume's argument (I claim to show in Chapter 8) is of very great importance, even though it is partly quite opposite to what Hume intended to teach us.

But the evaluation of an argument requires, at least if it is to be of any interest either philosophical or historical, that the argument be first of all correctly identified. The detailed identification of what Hume's argument for inductive scepticism actually was, therefore, is attempted in Part Two (Chapters 2-4). These three chapters will, I think, be found the most contentious in the book; but the later, evaluative chapters nevertheless depend entirely for their interest on the accuracy of the account which I have given in Chapters 2-4 of what Hume's argument for inductive scepticism in fact was.

My identification of this argument (and in consequence my evaluation of it) involves the identification of Hume's sceptical conclusion, as well as some of his premisses, as being *statements of logical probability*. In Parts Two and Three, therefore, I needed to be able to assume a number of things about propositions of that kind. It seemed advisable to state these things all in one place, and preferable to do so before I made any mention of induction, or of Hume, or of inductive scepticism. This is what I have done in the only chapter of Part One. The remarks assembled there about statements of logical probability are not at all original, except in matters of emphasis. Their substance can be found in Carnap, or in Keynes, or in other writers in the Keynes–Carnap tradition. At least within that tradition, nothing in Chapter 1 is even controversial.

Hume's scepticism about induction is quite interesting enough, even considered in itself, to justify the present inquiry. But it is very doubtful, of course, whether in historical fact there exists any sceptical view of induction other than Hume's. (There could of course be other arguments for Humean inductive scepticism, beside the one that Hume himself gave for it.) It is, at any rate, Humean inductive scepticism, and no other, which has dominated subsequent philosophical reflection on induction, especially in the present century. Thus in 1921 J. M. Keynes could write, at the end of 'Some Historical Notes on Induction', that 'Hitherto Hume has been master, only to be refuted in the manner of Diogenes and Dr. Johnson.'[1] And in 1966 Professor Wesley Salmon still finds it natural, as indeed it is, to organize a book on *The Foundations of Scientific Inference*[2] in the form of a discussion of various attempted 'answers' to Hume's inductive scepticism. Our inquiry has, therefore, by implication a much wider importance than would attach to a discussion of an argument of Hume, considered simply as such.

Still, it is no more than a historical fact (supposing it to be a fact) that inductive scepticism has been coextensive with *Hume's* inductive scepticism. The two are certainly not necessarily identical, and I wish to emphasize that it is the latter, not the former, which is the subject of this book. This limitation needs emphasis, because otherwise some of the claims made in the book will be apt to appear more general, and more positive, than they really are. This is especially true of the argument advanced in Chapter 5 section (*iii*), and I ask the reader to observe that what I claim for that argument is not, for example, that it is a justification of induction; but just that it is a refutation of Hume's scepticism about induction.

[1] *A Treatise on Probability* (London, 1921), p. 273. (Referred to hereafter as *Treatise*, except where the full title is needed in order to prevent confusion of Keynes's book with Hume's *Treatise*.)
[2] University of Pittsburgh Press, 1966.

Part One
SOME REMARKS ON PROBABILITY

1

CHIEFLY ON STATEMENTS OF LOGICAL PROBABILITY

(i) Principles and statements of probability

The theory of probability, on any interpretation of the word 'probability', contains propositions of two different kinds which it is most important to distinguish. One of these kinds is that which Carnap calls 'elementary statements of probability,'[1] and which I will call simply 'statements of probability'. The other kind I will call 'the principles' of probability.

A statement of probability is any categorical proposition which expresses a measurement, or more generally an assessment, not necessarily a correct one, of some particular probability or other. The principles of probability, on the other hand, do not themselves assess any probabilities, correctly or otherwise, but are general conditional propositions from which a statement of probability can be deduced when, but not before, other statements of probability have been asserted.

The relation which exists between statements, and the principles, of probability can best be made clear by an analogy with two kinds of propositions in geometry. When we consider any particular right-angled triangle, whether actual or imaginary, the Theorem of Pythagoras cannot itself, of course, tell us the length of any of the sides. Conjoined, however, with measurements of any two of the sides, the Theorem enables us to deduce the length of the third. In just the same way, the principles of probability, without statements of probability, are (to paraphrase Kant) empty; and statements of probability, without principles, are blind.

I speak of 'statements', and by contrast, of '*the* principles' of probability, for the following simple reason. The correct assessment

[1] *Logical Foundations of Probability* (Chicago University Press, 2nd edn., 1962), pp. 29–36. (Referred to hereafter as *Foundations*.)

of particular probabilities, and especially their numerical assessment, often presents great or even insuperable difficulty, and as a result people often disagree in their statements of probability. At least some of the statements of probability which are believed must, therefore, be false. But the general principles by which further probabilities are to be calculated, once some probabilities are supposed to have been correctly assessed to begin with, are, on the other hand, extremely well known and nowhere in dispute. They must, in fact, have been known, at least in an implicit way, for a very long time indeed; and in the present century, in particular, they have been reduced many times over, and in many different ways, to a system of axioms and theorems. These 'axioms and theorems of the calculus' of probability are what I call principles of probability. And I speak of *the* principles, because I intend to take for granted the truth of the familiar ones (and of course of no others). When I call a proposition a *statement* of probability, on the other hand, I will always intend to leave open the question whether or not it is a true one.

(ii) Factual probability and logical probability

Along with Carnap and many other recent philosophical writers on probability, I think that there are two different senses of 'probability', a factual one and a logical one.[2]

If this is so, then there are two theories of probability, and there are four kinds of propositions about probability which need to be distinguished. There are the principles of factual probability, and statements of factual probability; and again, there are the principles of logical probability, and statements of logical probability. What is factual about the theory of factual probability, and what is logical about the theory of logical probability, will not show forth, however, in connection with their respective principles; for the principles of factual probability and the principles of logical probability are alike in both being propositions of a non-factual kind. It is only in connection with statements of probability, therefore, that the difference between the theory of factual and the theory of logical probability shows itself.

A statement of factual probability is being made when and only when we assess the probability of one attribute in relation to a second attribute, which picks out a class of individuals in which the

[2] *Foundations*, Ch. II.

Factual probability and logical probability

first attribute may occur. Thus we may say, for example, that the probability of a radium atom decaying in a certain interval of time is $= \frac{1}{2}$; that the probability of throwing a 'four' with this die is $> \frac{1}{6}$; that the probability of a genetic mutation being beneficial is small; that the probability of a woman over thirty giving birth to twins is greater than the probability of a woman under thirty doing so; and so on. Such propositions clearly are assessments of probability, and equally clearly, they are propositions of a factual, contingent kind. Experience is needed, and is able, to confirm or to disconfirm them.

What factual probability *is*, need not detain us here. We need not even pause to inquire whether Carnap and many others are right in supposing that factual probability is to be analysed in terms of the relative frequency with which the one attribute occurs in the population of individuals picked out by the other. For my concern in this book is exclusively with the other, logical, theory of probability.

A statement of logical probability is being made when and only when we assess the probability of one proposition in relation to a second proposition, which picks out possible evidence for or against the first. Thus we may say, for example, that in relation to the evidence that the factual probability of throwing 'four' with this die is $= \frac{1}{6}$, the probability of the hypothesis, that John at his first trial with it will throw 'four', is $= \frac{1}{6}$; that the probability that Socrates is mortal, in relation to the evidence that Socrates is a man and all men are mortal, is > 0; that relative to the knowledge existing in the physical sciences in April 1970, the steady-state cosmological theory is less probable than the big-bang theory; that in relation to what has so far been observed of comets, the probability of the hypothesis that the next comet observed will have a low-density tail, is high; and so on.

Propositions such as these (whether true or false) clearly assess probability, but they are not propositions of a factual kind. Any one of them mentions two propositions, viz. the evidence and the hypothesis, the 'primary propositions', as Keynes called them,[3] of a statement of logical probability; and these, indeed (our interests being what in fact they are), will usually both be of a factual kind. But the assessment itself, of the probability of the hypothesis relative to the evidence, is a proposition of a different kind. What determines *its* truth or falsity is not the truth or falsity of its primary

[3] *Treatise*, p. 11.

propositions (and still less that of any other factual proposition), but just the relation between the two primary propositions. That relation is fully fixed once the content of each of the primary propositions is fixed; and what those contents are, is not a question of fact, but a question of meaning. Statements of logical as distinct from factual probability, therefore, are propositions of a kind, the truth or falsity of which experience is not able,[4] and not needed, to inform us.

So far I have followed Carnap in speaking of the subject of a statement of logical probability as being a certain ordered pair of propositions, and of these propositions respectively as 'evidence' and 'hypothesis'. In what follows, however, I intend to follow the usage of Keynes and many others,[5] including Carnap himself at times,[6] and to speak instead of the primary propositions as respectively 'premiss' and 'conclusion', and of the subject of the whole statement, correspondingly, as being the 'inference' or 'argument' from the former to the latter. Also, where Carnap speaks of the whole statement as 'assigning' a certain degree of logical probability 'to' its subject, I will speak of it always as 'assessing' the logical probability 'of' its subject. Clearly, the latter way of speaking accords better than the former with the possibility which, as I have said, I intend always to leave open when calling a proposition a statement of logical probability, that the proposition is a false one.

But what is that magnitude, the degree of which in a particular case a statement of logical probability assesses? What *is* logical probability?

According to Carnap, it is the degree of *confirmation* of the hypothesis h by the evidence e; and nothing in this book would need to be radically different from what it will be, if one were to adopt this answer. But a different answer is in fact suggested if we think of the primary propositions as the premiss and conclusion of an argument; and this answer is preferable because, among other things, it is closer to the conception which most of the writers in the tradition of Johnson, Keynes, and Carnap have had in mind, and also because it testifies to the continuity which exists between

---

[4] In section (*vii*) below, some minor exceptions will be noticed to what is said here.
[5] e.g. W. E. Johnson, *Logic* (Cambridge U.P., 1921–4), Part III, Ch. IV and Appendix; Keynes, *Treatise*, Parts I and II especially; H. Jeffreys, *Scientific Inference* (Cambridge U.P., 2nd edn., 1957), Ch. I; R. T. Cox, *The Algebra of Probable Inference* (Johns Hopkins Press, Baltimore, 1961), esp. Ch. I.
[6] *Foundations*, Appendix, pp. 567 ff.

these writers and the classical theorists of probability. This is, that logical probability is the degree of *conclusiveness* of the argument from e to h. That is, the degree of belief which a completely rational inferrer, who knew the premiss of the argument, and was influenced by nothing else, would have in its conclusion.

Some arguments, it is evident, have this property in the highest possible degree. A completely rational inferrer, that is to say, if he knew the premiss and were influenced by nothing else, would have in the conclusion the same degree of belief as he has in the premiss. All valid arguments, for example, have the highest possible degree of conclusiveness. (By calling an argument 'valid', I will always mean just that its premiss logically implies its conclusion.) It is equally evident that some other arguments do not have the highest possible degree of conclusiveness. A completely rational inferrer who knew the premiss of such an argument would have not the same but at most a lower degree of belief in its conclusion. (We are again assuming the influence of any other information he might have, beyond what the premiss contains, to be excluded.) No invalid arguments, for example, are of the highest degree of conclusiveness.

With these assertions, I think, everyone would agree, and they suffice to establish that conclusiveness is a property of arguments which is a magnitude at least in the minimal sense that some arguments have it in the highest possible degree and others do not. Deductive logic stops here, and is concerned to discriminate among arguments only according as they are, or are not, of the highest degree of conclusiveness. The theory of logical probability, on the other hand (or 'inductive logic' in Carnap's sense, but here see section (ix) below), is distinguished by the assertion that the conclusiveness of arguments is a magnitude in the further sense that degrees of it are ordered, at least to the extent that some of them lie between others. In other words, the fundamental thesis of the theory of logical probability (since some arguments certainly are valid and hence have the highest degree of conclusiveness) is that two arguments may be of unequal degrees of conclusiveness, even though both are invalid.

One must freely admit, or rather hasten to affirm, that 'degree of conclusiveness of an argument', even if a correct answer to 'What is logical probability?', is a far from ultimate answer to that question. Arguments certainly are not ultimate entities, and no magnitude which is characteristic of them can be ultimate either. Answers to this question which are more ultimate than the one I have given—more objective and 'logical', less epistemic—must exist; and indeed some already do exist, notably the answer which is given by Carnap in terms of the relation between the 'ranges' of two propositions. It is to be observed, however, that when writers attempt a more ultimate kind of answer than the one above to 'What is logical probability?', it is by reference to just such a non-ultimate conception of logical probability as I have given, and no other, that they test their own answers. Besides, no answer to this question, which is in terms of propositions and the relations between them, can hope to be an ultimate one. For propositions, although no doubt more ultimate than arguments, are certainly not ultimate entities. This reflection may be salutary, as reminding us how far we are from knowing what logical probability really is at bottom. On the other hand, it ought not to prevent us from admitting that there is a great deal which we already do know about logical probability.

One must distinguish, of course, between the fundamental idea—degree of conclusiveness of arguments—and the fundamental thesis of the theory of logical probability. Whether that thesis is true—whether, that is, there are unequal degrees of conclusiveness among invalid arguments—certainly can be doubted (and of course has been). That question will be under discussion, by implication, in Chapter 6 section (*iv*) below. But without the *idea* of degree of conclusiveness of arguments, it is not possible to understand the theory of logical probability, or indeed the classical theory of probability, at all.

(*iii*) *Kinds of statements of logical probability*

Within the theory of logical probability it is important to distinguish not only principles from statements of logical probability, but also different kinds of proposition within the latter class.

The statements of logical probability which generally receive most attention from writers on probability are what I will call 'numerical equalities'. That is, statements of the kind usually abbreviated $P(h, e) = r$, where e and h are premiss- and conclusion-propositions respectively, and r is a number between 0 and 1 (limits included): which assert, of course, that the probability of the argument from e to h is equal to r.

Statements of logical probability are sometimes spoken of as 'measuring' the logical probability of the argument (or ordered pair

Kinds of statements of logical probability

of propositions) which is their subject. This way of speaking is rather too apt to suggest, what need by no means be true, 'correctly measuring'; but otherwise it is appropriate enough, when the statement in question is a numerical equality. But numerical equalities, while they are the strongest and therefore the most interesting, are far from being the only kind of statements of logical probability; and there are other, weaker, kinds which, except in an intolerably extended sense of 'measure', could not be said to measure logical probability at all.

First, there are numerical *in*equalities, i.e. statements of the kind: $P(A, B) > \frac{1}{5}$, $P(C, D) < 1$, etc. (The capital letters are used here, for brevity, in place of concrete propositions.) Statements of this kind are weaker than numerical equalities, since, while any numerical equality entails infinitely many numerical inequalities, no conjunction of inequalities entails even one equality. And, it will be of importance later to note, among numerical inequalities, those which say of the logical probability of a certain argument only that it is less than the maximum ($P(C, D) < 1$), or that it is more than the minimum ($P(F, E) > 0$), are the weakest of all. For each of these excludes only one numerical equality, while every other inequality excludes infinitely many equalities.

There are other weaker kinds of statements of logical probability, however, which are not numerical at all, but purely comparative. That is, they say, of the logical probability of a certain argument, only that it is equal to the logical probability of a certain other argument: $P(A, B) = P(C, D)$ for example. Obviously, there are also inequalities of this purely comparative kind. The relative weakness of comparative, as compared with numerical, statements of logical probability appears from the fact that while a conjunction of numerical inequalities will often entail a comparative statement, no conjunction of comparatives suffices to entail even one numerical inequality.

The importance, despite their weakness, of comparative assessments of logical probability was first stressed by Keynes, and he rightly attached a special importance to a certain sub-class of comparative statements to which he gave the name of 'judgements of (ir)relevance'.[7] A judgement of irrelevance is a comparative equality in which the two arguments mentioned have the same conclusion, while the premiss of one of them entails, without being

---
[7] *Treatise*. See its index under 'Irrelevance'.

entailed by, the premiss of the other. Thus '$P(A, B) = P(A, B.C)$' (or 'The argument from C and B to A has the same probability as the argument to A from B alone') asserts the 'irrelevance' of C to A (relative to B); the contrary inequalities assert the 'favourable' and 'unfavourable' relevance, respectively, of C to A (relative to B).

Besides numerical and comparative equalities and inequalities, there are vague, but common and useful, 'classificatory' statements of logical probability. As when, for example, we say of a certain logical probability, only that it is 'low', or 'high', or 'considerable', or 'negligible', etc.

Statements of all these kinds are certainly used to assess the conclusiveness of arguments; although numerical equalities alone of them could properly be said to measure it. And assessments of all these kinds—numerical, comparative, and classificatory—are of course made of factual, as well as of logical, probabilities.

(iv) Greater and less generality among statements of logical probability

Statements of logical probability, whether numerical or of any other kind, can be less or more general. One will be less general than another if, in making it, we assess the conclusiveness of a single argument, or of a certain class of arguments; while in making the other, we assess the conclusiveness of another class of arguments which properly includes the first class, or includes the single argument as a member.

Thus, for example, 'P(Socrates is mortal, Socrates is a man and all men are mortal) $= 1$' is a less general statement of logical probability than 'P(x is G, x is F, and all F are G) $= 1$'. In fact the first assesses the conclusiveness of only a single argument. Any such statement of logical probability I will call 'singular'; any other, 'general'.

Any general statement of logical probability will require the employment of universally quantified variable expressions of one or more kinds. (The above example of a general statement employs both individual and predicate variables.) In writing general statements of logical probability, universal quantification of variables is usually left tacit (as it was, again, in the above example).

Many statements of logical probability are so very general that propositional variables are required for their expression; and these, too, have to be understood as tacitly universally quantified. But a statement which made the same assessment, $P(h, e) = r$, for every

Generality in statements of logical probability

value of h and for every value of e, would of course be ludicrously false. Consequently, a statement of logical probability employing propositional variables (unless it is a ludicrously false one) will always be accompanied by an indication of some limitation on the range of values which at least one of the variables is intended to take. For example, '$P(h, e) = 1$ for any contingent e and tautological h'; 'If h is a universal empirical proposition and e is observational, $P(h, e) < 1$', etc.

(v) *The commonness of statements of logical probability*

The contemporary theory of logical probability, it must be admitted, is something of a specialism even within the specialism which is philosophy. The standard abbreviations adopted for statements of logical probability tend especially to invest those statements with an air of technicality. For this reason among others, it deserves to be stressed that statements of logical probability are not an out-of-the-way kind of proposition, or of interest only to a few contemporary specialists. They are in fact as common as daylight, and of interest to everyone.

Certainly, philosophers and logicians at all periods have been much engaged in making assessments of the degree of conclusiveness of arguments, and even in making numerical assessments. For they constantly make, concerning arguments, judgements of validity and judgements of invalidity; and these are numerical equalities and inequalities respectively. To judge the argument from B to A valid is to assess its conclusiveness as being of the maximum degree, i.e. $P(A, B) = 1$; while to judge it invalid is to affirm that $P(A, B) < 1$.

Far more common still are the weaker kinds of statement of logical probability which were distinguished from the numerical ones in section *(iii)* above; and the making of these is not even more characteristic of philosophers than of non-philosophers. The scientist, the judge, the detective, and indeed any intelligent person, is constantly being called on to decide whether comparative statements of logical probability are true: whether, that is, $P(h_1, e_1) = P(h_2, e_2)$, or not. Even more commonly than other kinds of comparative assessment, we all make many judgements of (ir)relevance. In fact, any one who, with his inferential capacity in working order, has new information constantly flowing in upon him (as we, for example, have from perception) must make countless judgements of (ir)relevance. For such an inferrer has constantly to consider whether the degree of conclusiveness of his 'old' inference from e_1 to h is the same as that from $e_1.e_2$ to h, where e_2 is his new information; i.e. whether $P(h, e_1) = P(h, e_1.e_2)$. For most of his hypotheses h, and most of his old pieces of information e_1 and most of his new pieces of information e_2, he will in fact, presumably, make the judgement of *ir*relevance. But this itself suffices to show that assessments of logical probability constitute an immense fabric of belief, even with the least reflective among us.

Where the reflective and educated differ from those who are neither is not in making assessments of logical probability at all, or in making more of them, but in the greater generality of many of the assessments that they do make. The ordinary man may be unfailingly accurate in the assessments he makes of the conclusiveness of single arguments, but it is the mark of the reflective mind to assess whole classes of arguments at once: to judge (truly) that every syllogism in Barbara is valid; to judge (falsely) that every case of 'affirming the consequent' is invalid; to judge (truly) that $P(h, e_1) = P(h, e_1.e_2)$ for every contingent h and e_1 and every tautological e_2; and so on. But whether true or false, singular or general, assessments of conclusiveness are constantly being made, by the learned and the vulgar alike.

Even the kinds of statement of logical probability which were enumerated in section *(iii)* above, however, are far from exhausting the language which we use to assess conclusiveness. They are, rather, only the tip of the iceberg. Far more common than all of those kinds of statement put together are assessments of the conclusiveness of inferences which are expressed in the utterly untechnical terminology of one proposition's being 'some grounds', or 'slight foundation', or 'no reason', etc., for belief in another. It is in such language as this that most of the assessing of the conclusiveness of inferences is carried on, at the present time as at earlier times, and by philosophers as well as by non-philosophers.

Such language is very vague, of course. Yet it can be used so as to convey the same thing as one of the more definite kinds of statements of logical probability which were discussed above. For example, if a writer, to express his assessment of the conclusiveness of two arguments, repeatedly uses the same phrase, then, however untechnical and vague it may be, we will clearly be entitled to ascribe to him belief in a comparative equality concerning those two arguments.

The commonness of statements of logical probability

We will meet a remarkable instance of just this sort in Part Two below. It will involve me in attributing to an eighteenth-century writer certain statements of logical probability. Such an attribution is apt at first to seem absurdly anachronistic. But there can be no anachronism about such an attribution, if what has been said in this section, and the two preceding ones, is true. The attribution may be erroneous, of course, but that is another matter, to be decided on the basis of the texts. And even the chance of error will be somewhat diminished by the fact that the eighteenth-century writer in question was a philosopher, and consequently was engaged even more often than most men in assessing the conclusiveness of arguments.

(vi) 'Initial' logical probabilities and 'regularity'
It will be important later in this book to make assessments of the degree of conclusiveness of certain arguments from tautological premisses. Such an assessment I will call, following Carnap, a statement of 'initial'[8] logical probability; and it will be found convenient to follow Carnap's practice of letting the propositional variable 't' take only tautological values when it occurs as a primary proposition in a statement of logical probability. Thus, a statement of initial logical probability will, when abbreviated, always begin $P(h, t) \ldots$; and conversely, whatever begins so will be a statement of initial logical probability.

Since most of the arguments in which we are actually interested are, as I have observed earlier, from (as well as to) a factual proposition, we are apt to find the idea of statements of initial logical probability strange at first. Yet initial logical probabilities do exist. Indeed, unless the principles of logical probability are supposed to have an application much more restricted than has ever, so far as I know, been ascribed to them, then for every h and e, $P(h, e) = \dfrac{P(h.e, t)}{P(e, t)}$ (by the conjunction ('multiplication') principle, and the principle that logically equivalent propositions can always be substituted for one another *salva probabilitate* in statements and principles of logical probability; along with the equivalence of 'e' and '$e.t$' for any e). Every logical probability, in other words, requires the existence of at least two initial logical probabilities.

But there is no need for us thus to infer that initial logical probabilities exist. For there are a good many assessments of the logical

[8] *Foundations*, § 57.

probability of arguments from tautological premises which we know the truth of directly, as directly as we know any statements of logical probability whatever. Some of them, moreover, are of very great generality. For example, '$P(h, t) = 0$ for any self-contradictory h'. Or again, 'For any contingent h, $P(h, t) < 1$'.

This last proposition is essentially Carnap's requirement of 'regularity' for adequate measures of logical probability.[9] It is, clearly, such a 'requirement', though not in the sense of being in the least an arbitrary stipulation; only in the sense of being very general, not usually inferred from anything else, and true. For to deny it would be to affirm that some contingent propositions can be inferred with the highest possible degree of conclusiveness from a tautology.

Statements of logical probability asserting $P(h, e) < 1$ for some limited range of values of h and e, I have earlier called 'judgements of invalidity'. I propose to call judgements of invalidity $P(h, t) < 1$ where h is contingent, 'judgements of regularity'. They will prove especially important in Part Three below.

(vii) The non-factual character of statements of logical probability

The logical probability of an argument is its degree of conclusiveness; that is, the degree of belief which would attend its conclusion in a completely rational inferrer who knew the premiss and was influenced by nothing else. What this degree is, in any particular case, will depend on the content of the premiss and conclusion, and on nothing else; and what their contents are, is a question of meaning, not of fact. Statements of logical probability, consequently, are not propositions of a factual, or more particularly, of an empirical kind. Consequently neither their truth nor their falsity can be discovered by experience.

All this was said in section *(ii)* above. We have now to notice, with respect to the final conclusion just drawn, first, some exceptions (essentially just one exception) to it; and second, an important consequence of its being, with this exception, true.

Within the class of all statements of logical probability, consider the sub-class consisting of numerical equalities, $P(h, e) = r$. Within this sub-class, consider just the further sub-class in which the number r is 1, or is 0. Then all the statements which we are con-

---

[9] Cf. *Foundations*, pp. 294 ff. Strictly, of course, for Carnap this requirement is confined to measures of logical probability for languages containing a finite number of individual constants.

Statements of logical probability are non-factual 17

sidering are, or are equivalent to, judgements of validity, $P(h, e) = 1$. Within this class, consider just the further sub-class which consists of *false* judgements of validity. Now, the proposition $\sim h.e$, consisting of the premiss of the argument which is being assessed, conjoined with the negation of the conclusion, is certainly inconsistent with the false judgement of validity $P(h, e) = 1$. This proposition, moreover, may happen to be an observational one, in virtue of the content of e and $\sim h$, if $P(h, e) = 1$ is singular. And if $P(h, e) = 1$ is general, it will usually be possible to choose values of the predicate or propositional variables in h and e in such a way as to construct an observational counter-example, $\sim h.e$, to the judgement of validity. Sometimes at least, therefore, false judgements of validity are inconsistent with some observation-statement; i.e. are falsifiable. Some statements of logical probability at least, therefore, are such that their falsity can in principle be learned from experience.

For precisely the same reasons, some statements of logical probability are such that their truth can in principle be learned from experience: viz. the contradictories of the statements just mentioned. True judgements of invalidity (that is to say, $P(h, e) < 1$ or equivalent statements) are at least sometimes deducible from some observation-statement; i.e. are verifiable. (This 'second' exception to the generalization which I made above is of course only apparently different from the first: for the falsifiability of a false judgement of validity differs only verbally from the verifiability of a true judgement of invalidity.)

But the restrictions which were laid down in the last paragraph but one were all necessary in order to make possible even this (essentially single) exception to my generalization. Where the number r is not extreme (1 or 0), $P(h, e) = r$ is never falsifiable: for then it is not inconsistent with $\sim h.e$, even if that proposition is observational. And if the judgement of validity $P(h, e) = 1$ is not false, but true, then of course $\sim h.e$ is self-contradictory and consequently not an observation-statement. All other numerical equalities or inequalities, therefore (i.e. where the condition of extremeness or the condition of falsity fails), are neither falsifiable nor verifiable. The same is true *a fortiori* of all those statements of logical probability which are not even numerical, but merely comparative or classificatory.

Since the vast majority of statements of logical probability cannot have their truth or their falsity determined by experience, how *is* their truth-value to be determined?

One can prove the truth of a statement of logical probability, by validly deriving it, via the principles of logical probability, from other statement(s) of logical probability of which the truth is intuitively obvious. And one can prove the falsity of a statement of logical probability by validly deriving from it, via the principles, some other statement(s) of logical probability of which the falsity is intuitively obvious. These are the only ways in which any statement of logical probability (other than the exceptions just discussed) can have its truth-value determined indirectly, i.e. by inference. And it will be obvious that the possibility of such indirect determinations of truth-value depends on there being some statements of logical probability, the truth or falsity of which can be known *directly*.

In this sense, almost every application of the theory of logical probability depends in the end on intuitive assessments of logical probability.[10] This is not at all to admit that statements of logical probability are, in any important sense whatever, 'subjective'. It is not at all to admit, in particular, that hardly any false statement of logical probability can 'really' be proved false. For it would certainly prove the falsity of a given statement of logical probability if it were possible to derive from it, via the principles, $P(x$ is G, x is F, and all F are $G) = \frac{1}{2}$, for example; or $P(x$ is G, x is F, and all F are $G) = P(x$ is F, x is G, and all F are $G)$; or $P(x$ is not G, x is F, and all F are $G) > P(x$ is not G, x is $F)$; or a violation of regularity $P(h, t) = 1$ for some contingent h; or any one of very many other equally obviously false consequences. Yet our knowledge that these consequences *are* false rests on no factual (and in particular no empirical) foundation whatever.

Reliance on intuition, in the sense in which it is admitted here, is not even peculiar to the theory of logical probability, but is equally characteristic of deductive logic. For deductive logic is concerned principally with true judgements of validity; and as we have seen, the truth of a judgement of validity, like the truth of most other statements of logical probability, is not discoverable empirically.[11]

[10] Cf. Carnap, 'Inductive Logic and Inductive Intuition', in Lakatos, ed., *The Problem of Inductive Logic* (North-Holland, Amsterdam, 1968). Popper, in his comments on this essay in the same volume, points out in effect that (unlike other statements of logical probability, some) judgements of validity can have their falsity discovered (not only intuitively but) by empirical counter-example. See ibid., pp. 286, 296–7.

[11] This, I suggest, is the important element of truth in the thesis of symmetry, as between deductive logic and 'inductive logic' in Carnap's sense, which is maintained by Carnap, and criticized by Popper, in the volume referred to in the preceding footnote.

Statements of logical probability are non-factual

Statements of logical probability of which the truth is discoverable empirically, we have seen, are confined to the small minority which consists of true judgements of invalidity. But of course, even when a statement belongs to this minority, its truth, even if known and capable of being discovered empirically, need not have been in fact discovered empirically. The truth, for example, of P(x is F, x is G, and all F are G) $<$ 1 (the invalidity of the 'undistributed middle' for logically independent predicates) may become known to us by the aid of a counter-example to the contrary false judgement of validity. But it need not be inferred from such an actual case. Nor need it be inferred from anything else; for its truth may be intuitively obvious without inference. Most true judgements of invalidity, at least when they concern simple arguments very obviously invalid, are in fact discovered directly.

It will be worthwhile to emphasize that, in addition, even among true judgements of invalidity, there are indefinitely many the truth of which can only be discovered non-empirically. These are the true judgements of invalidity which are singular, and which concern an argument of which either the conclusion h is true, or the premiss e false in fact. Clearly, in such cases the possibility is logically excluded of learning the truth of P(h, e) $<$ 1 by finding that in fact $\sim h.e$. The statement of logical probability, if known, must be known directly by intuition; or, if it is not known directly but inferred, it must be inferred from other statements of logical probability some at least of which are known intuitively. As an interesting special case it may be observed that, since h is contingent if and only if its negation is contingent, half at least of all singular judgements of regularity can be discovered to be true only non-empirically.

(viii) *What the theory of logical probability enables us to do*

The two kinds of propositions—statements, and the principles, of logical probability—as well as excluding one another, exhaust the theory of logical probability. (Purely mathematical propositions 'belong' to the theory of logical probability only in the external and auxiliary sense in which they also belong to, say, physics.) Consequently, what the theory of logical probability enables us to do is just what the principles, conjoined with some statements of logical probability, enable us to do. And that is, to derive further statements of logical probability.

This does not sound as though it could be very instructive; and under some circumstances, it would not be. Suppose, for example, that a man made just one statement of logical probability, and never made another. Or suppose that a man made many such statements, but all of them singular, and about arguments of utterly unrelated subject-matter, so that the statements of logical probability to which he committed himself had no primary propositions in common. Then, in either of these cases, application of the principles, in order to derive other statements of logical probability, could not furnish the materials for any criticism of his original statements; for all of the consequences derivable from them are statements which, by the hypotheses, he neither affirms nor denies.

Our actual case is far otherwise, however, if what I have said earlier in this chapter is true: viz. that we make very many, and many of these very general, assessments of logical probability. Under these circumstances there is the possibility that the principles will bring to light an inconsistency in our assessments which would never have been disclosed except by tracing those assessments into their remoter consequences. And the likelihood of there being such inconsistencies is the greater, of course, the more numerous, and the more general, our assessments are to begin with.

More generally, however, the theory of logical probability is instructive because it can bring to light consequences of our assessments of logical probability which are unforeseen, and which, even if not inconsistent with any of our other assessments, are nevertheless surprising and unwelcome. Let us call an assessment of the conclusiveness of a certain class of arguments 'the natural' assessment, if it is that which is or would be made by almost all men; and let us call an assessment a 'sceptical' one, if it ascribes, to a certain class of arguments, less conclusiveness than the natural assessment does; if it ascribes more, a 'credulous' assessment. Natural assessments exist for many classes of arguments, though of course (since no one could consider all possible arguments) not for all. Now, an assessment of certain arguments which is either sceptical or credulous will entail, in virtue of the principles of logical probability, further assessments, either credulous or sceptical, of other arguments (so long as the natural assessments are themselves consistent). To take the simplest sort of illustration: if for a certain class of arguments, i.e. for a certain limited range of values of h and e, a man makes a *sceptical* assessment $P(h, e) = r$, then the negation principle

What the theory of logical probability enables us to do

commits him to making a *credulous* assessment, $P(\sim h, e) = 1-r$, of the class of arguments from e to not-h.

This kind of service which the principles of logical probability, combined with our statements, can perform for us, is particularly important. For philosophers are rather too apt to think that they can depart from the natural assessments of inferences, in the direction of scepticism, in a more piecemeal fashion than is really possible. The principles of probability can show us that our scepticism about one class of arguments must be extended to classes of arguments about which we had never dreamed of being sceptical, or again, must be compensated for by an embarrassing credulity concerning some other arguments. (A striking instance of the latter kind will be discussed in Chapter 5 below.) This, rather more often than the disclosure of an outright inconsistency in our assessments, is the valuable kind of instruction which the theory of logical probability can afford us.

(ix) *Logical probability and inductive inference*

As the word 'inductive' has almost always been used, inductive inference, whatever else it may be, is at any rate inference from experience. An inference, that is, is not called 'inductive' unless its premiss is observational: consisting of reports of (actual or possible) past or present observations. Thus, the class of inferences of which the following is a paradigm ('Bernoullian' inferences as I will call them), is not inductive. 'The factual probability of a human birth being male is = 0·51, and there were a large number of human births in Australia between 1960 and 1970, so the relative frequency of male births in Australia at that time was close to 0·51.'[12] The inference, on the other hand, which has the major premiss of the above inference as its conclusion, and the above conclusion and minor premiss as its premisses, is inductive; or at any rate, it satisfies the condition stated above as being necessary for an inference to be inductive. For the statement of factual probability is not observational, whereas the statements about the number of births in

[12] Inferences of this kind become statistical inferences, of course, as soon as the probability referred to in the major premiss is given an interpretation in terms of relative frequency. They become, in particular, inferences from the relative frequency of an attribute in a certain population to its relative frequency in a large sample from that population. For this reason the name 'Bernoullian inference' will be applied later in this book to inferences of this latter kind as well, and also to the closely related kind of inference in which both the minor premiss and the conclusion are singular.

Australia between 1960 and 1970, and about the observed relative frequency of males among them, *are* observational.

What class of inferences is to be understood in this book by the phrase 'inductive inferences' will be specified more narrowly in the next chapter. But the restriction already mentioned—that the premiss be observational—is sufficient to ensure that inductive inferences constitute a quite special class of inferences, and as such have no more intimate a connection with the theory of logical probability than any other special class of inferences. No more, for example, than Bernoullian inferences have. The theory of logical probability is no more especially about inferences from observational premisses than it is especially about inferences, for example, from a premiss which includes a statement of factual probability. The principles of logical probability are perfectly general.[13] Not only do they not assess the conclusiveness of, they in no way mention, any particular class of inferences such as the inductive ones. Of course, once some assessment has been made of the conclusiveness of some or all inferences from experience, though not before, the principles will enable us to derive therefrom other assessments of other inferences; not all of which will have observational premisses, and not all of which, therefore, can be inductive. But of course that is neither more nor less than the kind of thing which the principles will do for us in connection with any other particular class of inferences.

It seems advisable to insist on this, in view of the great amount of confusion which, in about the last 100 years, has come to surround the relation between the two topics, induction and probability. (What has brought these two topics into close connection, why the confusion about their relation should have arisen at all, and why it should have arisen just when it did, will, I hope, be explained by Chapter 8 below.)

This is also the place to comment on Carnap's highly idiosyncratic usage of the word 'inductive'. This departs from the main stream of usage of the word, once by omitting something, and once by adding something not present before. First, Carnap omits from the sense of 'inductive' the descriptive element, remarked on above, which confines it to inferences from observational premisses. And

---

[13] The only inferences which the theory of probability is prevented by its principles from taking account of, are those from self-contradictory premisses. Cf. Carnap, *Foundations*, pp. 295 ff.

second, he imports into the meaning of the word an evaluative element which was lacking before. During most of the last 300 years, it was no part of the function of the word 'inductive' to convey any assessment whatever of the conclusiveness of any argument from observational premises. But as Carnap uses 'inductive', in contrast with 'deductive', it is at least part of the meaning of calling an inference 'inductive', that it is invalid. One result of this second departure from the main stream of usage is, as we will see in Chapters 7 and 8, the trivialization of an important truth. The result of the two departures combined is that Carnap regularly calls the great enterprise, of which he is himself the chief architect, by a seriously misleading name. What he calls the construction of a system of 'inductive logic' is in reality the construction of a system of non-demonstrative logic in general, or simply, the theory of logical probability.[14]

In speaking, for most of this chapter, about logical probability, therefore, I have been speaking about 'inductive logic' in Carnap's sense. But if we take 'inductive' in its usual sense—in which, applied to inferences, the word *does* convey a limitation on the nature of the premisses, and does *not* convey any assessment of the conclusiveness of the inference—then it will be evident that I have so far said or assumed nothing about inductive inference. In particular I have not said or implied anything about the degree of conclusiveness of any arguments from experience; any more than I have, say, about the degree of conclusiveness of Bernoullian inferences. The degree of conclusiveness of inductive inferences is, in fact, the subject of most of the remainder of this book; but it is a question that is entirely untouched by anything said so far.

---

[14] Carnap's usage of 'inductive', however idiosyncratic, is clear, and it ought to have been possible for him to adhere to it consistently. But as so often happens, normal usage reasserts its rights, and Carnap is sometimes led to say something which is true only in the normal sense of 'inductive', quite false in his own sense of that word. Thus in his article 'On Inductive Logic', Carnap says that the evidence-sentence *e*, mentioned in any statement of logical probability, '*is usually a report on the results of our observations*'. (*Philosophy of Science*, 1945, p. 72. My italics.) But taking 'inductive logic' in his broad sense, this remark is simply baseless and untrue. It can only be regarded as an inconsistent concession to the main stream of usage o f 'inductive'.

Part Two
HUME'S ARGUMENT FOR INDUCTIVE
SCEPTICISM: IDENTIFICATION

2
ITS STRUCTURE AND CONTENT

(i) Preliminary textual identification of the argument

Hume certainly thought of himself as having advanced, about inductive inferences, some proposition of a sceptical kind; of a kind, that is, which is shocking to common beliefs, and unfavourable to men's pretensions to knowledge. Nearly all of Hume's readers must also have thought that he did so. I shall therefore take this point as granted. It is safe to assume, further, that Hume did not merely assert this sceptical thesis about induction, but argued for it. The question in this Part of the book is, what was his argument?

It would be idle, of course, to try to answer this question by looking in Hume's writings for an argument for 'inductive scepticism' *eo nomine*. Hume does, indeed, have much to say about different kinds of scepticism, though only one of these kinds will concern us. But he does not use the words 'inductive' or 'induction'.[1] Where we would find it natural to employ the adjective 'inductive', Hume speaks of arguments, or inferences, or reasoning(s) 'from experience';[2] or 'from causes or effects';[3] or even 'concerning matter of fact'.[4] The arguments which he discusses under these headings, however, are all (with one possible exception),[5] ones which we would call inductive.

[1] With the solitary exception that 'induction' occurs once, in the Appendix to the *Treatise*, p. 628. Even here, however, Hume seems to use the word *not* of argument from observational premisses. (The reference here is to the Selby-Bigge edition of *A Treatise of Human Nature* (Oxford U.P., 1888). All my page-references to the *Treatise*, and to the first *Enquiry* (*An Enquiry concerning Human Understanding*, Oxford U.P., 1894) are to the Selby-Bigge editions of those works.)
[2] *An Abstract of a Treatise of Human Nature* (in Flew, ed., *Hume on Human Nature and the Understanding*, Collier Books, New York, 1962), p. 293. (All my page-references to the *Abstract* are to this edition.)
[3] *Treatise*, p. 124.   [4] *Abstract*, p. 292.
[5] Viz. the class of arguments, whatever it is, which Hume discusses in section xi of Book I Part III of the *Treatise*, and in the third paragraph of the corresponding section vi of the *Enquiry*. See the Appendix below, section *(ii)*.

Arguments from experience are, of course, the central topic of Hume's philosophy 'of the understanding'. But, it should be observed, Hume never discusses all kinds of inductive arguments together, as a class. Instead, he breaks up this class of arguments into a number of different 'species of reasoning',[6] and discusses each 'species' separately. And he devotes to just one of these special classes of arguments from experience more attention than he does to all the rest combined.

That one is the kind of reasoning which Hume called 'the inference from the impression to the idea',[7] 'when' (or 'after') 'we have had experience'—a 'long, uniform'[8] experience—of the conjunction of one observable property with another. The following example, which is based on one of Hume's, will serve us as a paradigm of the class of arguments which he treats under this heading. 'This is a flame, and all of the many flames observed in the past have been hot, so, this is hot.' The first part of the premiss here corresponds, of course, to Hume's 'impression'; the second part, to a long uniform 'experience'; the conclusion, to Hume's 'idea'. It would be intolerably cumbrous if I were to continue to refer to arguments of this kind as 'inferences from the impression to the idea, when we have had experience'. Instead I will call them 'predictive-inductive' inferences. Predictive-inductive inferences, then, constitute that 'species of reasoning' which occupied Hume's attention in the greater part of Book I Part III of the *Treatise*; in the central sections iv and v of the *Enquiry*; and in the *Abstract*.

This is also the only kind of inductive inference concerning which Hume ever advanced a clear argument which ends in a sceptical conclusion. For, on the one hand, Hume never discusses explicitly (what it sometimes seems to be thought he discussed exclusively) *universal*-inductive inferences: the class of inferences, that is, of which 'All of the many flames observed in the past have been hot, so, all flames are hot' will serve us as a paradigm. And on the other hand, the other kinds of argument from experience which he does discuss are treated by Hume at any length only in sections xi–xiii of the *Treatise* Book I Part III: three sections which have been very much neglected by students of Hume, and on the whole, in

[6] *Treatise*, p. 124.
[7] The title of section vi of Book I Part III of the *Treatise*.
[8] The phrases here placed in quotation marks will be found repeated, with minor variations, in all the passages in the *Treatise*, *Abstract*, and *Enquiry* which are to be specified in the next paragraph but three.

Preliminary textual identification of the argument

view of their defects, justly neglected. In this book, consideration of these sections is relegated to the Appendix. This is the more justified, in that Hume says quite clearly that he has no fresh argument to offer, concerning the kinds of inference considered in those sections, beyond what he has already advanced concerning the predictive-inductive inference.[9]

Thus it is not about all inductive inferences, but only predictive-inductive ones, that there exists an argument in Hume which is explicit and clear, and which ends in a sceptical conclusion. What we must first attend to, therefore, is his argument for the limited conclusion which we may call 'predictive-inductive scepticism'. For this conclusion Hume certainly does advance a clear argument in the *Treatise*, and one which, at least by the time that he wrote the *Abstract*, he realized was 'the chief argument of that book';[10] as it was also to be of the first *Enquiry*. It is this argument which will occupy us throughout this chapter and the next, and, in a generalized form, for the rest of this book.

But Hume's argument for scepticism about the predictive-inductive inference was never presented by him as a free-standing one. It was, in fact, always presented as one stage, the second, of a longer argument. The first stage of this longer argument has as its subject-matter a different kind of inference. This is what Hume calls, by way of contrast with the subject of the second stage, 'the inference from the impression to the idea', 'before we have had' (or 'without', or 'independent of') 'experience'. That is, taking the 'experience' (of the conjunction of heat with flame) out of the premiss of the predictive-inductive inference, the class of inferences of which 'This is a flame, so, this is hot' will serve as a paradigm. I will call such inferences, '*a priori*' inferences. It will prove to be very important for an understanding of the second stage of the longer argument, i.e. of Hume's argument for predictive-inductive scepticism, that we should take into account this earlier stage of his argument, concerning *a priori* inferences.

This two-stage argument is the central feature of Hume's philosophy of the understanding, and is to be found fully-fledged at the following places in the texts. In the *Abstract*, stage 1 of the argument, about the *a priori* inference, begins at the foot of p. 292;

[9] Cf. *Treatise*, p. 126, the sentence beginning 'Here we may repeat . . .' The same thing is implied on p. 139, by the passage beginning 'And no doubt . . .'
[10] This quotation is from the full title of the *Abstract*.

stage 2 of the argument, about the predictive-inductive inference, begins with the new paragraph just below the middle of p. 293; and the whole argument ends with the second-last paragraph of p. 294. In the *Enquiry* the relevant section is iv, 'Sceptical Doubts concerning the Operations of the Understanding'. Part I of this section is an extended presentation of stage 1 of the argument; Part II of the section is an equally extended presentation of stage 2 of the argument. The essential substance of Hume's argument about the predictive-inductive inference (i.e. stage 2) runs from near the top of p. 35 to near the top of p. 36. But the sceptical conclusion of stage 2 is not explicitly drawn in the *Enquiry* until the next section v, 'Sceptical Solution of these Doubts', pp. 42–3. In the *Treatise* the relevant sections are Book I Part III sections ii–viii, especially vi, 'Of the inference from the impression to the idea'. Here stage 1, concerning the *a priori* inference, is dispatched in the first paragraph of the section. Stage 2, concerning the predictive-inductive inference, begins with the second paragraph, p. 87; is resumed with the new paragraph at the foot of p. 88; and is essentially concluded with the second paragraph of p. 90.

The account of Hume's argument which I give below is, as it were, a composite photograph of all these different versions. The version in the *Abstract* is in most respects the best, however, and it is that to which my account of the argument corresponds most closely.

Hume is, of course, a very repetitive writer, and one can find his argument about the predictive-inductive inference sketched in many other places in his writings besides those just mentioned.[11]

(ii) The structure of the argument, and its content in the language of Hume

For the identification of an argument as complex as Hume's is, it is almost essential to separate the structure from the content of the argument. The best way to effect this separation seems to be to compile a 'dictionary' of the propositional elements of the argument, and to correlate them with the elements of a 'structure-diagram' of the argument.[12] This is what is done below for Hume's argument. The representation will be found self-explanatory, except perhaps that it needs to be emphasized that the arrow has no evaluative significance whatever. We are here trying just to identify a man's

---

[11] Cf. also section (i) of the Appendix below.
[12] This invaluable device has been borrowed from my friend, and former teacher and colleague, Professor J. L. Mackie.

argument, and $p \to q$, for example, means simply that p was in fact offered as a ground for believing q.

Dictionary of the elements of Hume's argument[13]

Stage 1

(a) Whatever is intelligible, is possible.

(b) That the inference from an impression (e.g. of flame) to an idea (e.g. of heat), *prior to* experience of the appropriate constant conjunction, should have its premiss true and conclusion false, is an intelligible supposition.

(c) That supposition is possible.

(d) The inference from the impression to the idea, prior to experience, is not one which reason engages us to make.

Stage 2

(e) Probable arguments all presuppose that unobserved (e.g. future) instances resemble observed ones.

(f) That there is this resemblance, is a proposition concerning matter of fact and existence.

(g) That proposition (i.e. the thesis of resemblance) cannot be proved by any demonstrative arguments.

(h) Any arguments for the thesis of resemblance must be probable ones.

(i) Any probable argument for that thesis would be circular.

(j) Even *after* we have had experience of the appropriate constant conjunction, it is not reason (but custom, etc.) which determines us to infer the idea (e.g. of heat) from the impression (e.g. of flame).

Structure-diagram of Hume's argument

Stage 1

Stage 2

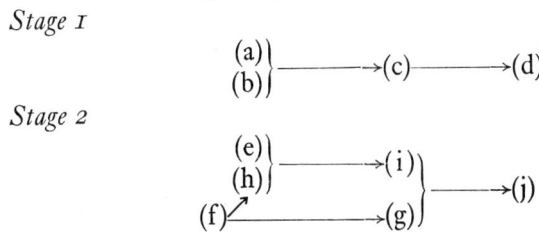

[13] In the *Philosophical Review* for April 1965 I published an account of Hume's argument which is very like the one given here, except in one vital respect. This is, that I there failed to distinguish between what later in this book will be called the *fallibilist consequence* of stage 2 of the argument, and the *sceptical conclusion* which Hume actually drew. I published another account of Hume's argument which is free from this defect in the *Australasian Journal of Philosophy* for May 1970.

Even if this account of the structure of Hume's argument is correct, it does not follow at all that the content of his argument needs no elucidation. The opposite is in fact the case. The language of the elements of the above dictionary is substantially that of Hume himself, and at certain points especially that language, as we will see in the next section, is rather deceptively different from what we would use to convey the same meaning. There is, however, one extremely important feature of the argument which, if my representation of it is correct, emerges already.

This is, the way in which the conclusion of the second stage of the argument reiterates or 'echoes' that of the first stage. For it can be seen already that the conclusion (d), which in stage 1 Hume drew concerning the *a priori* inference, is in its content the same as the conclusion (j) which in stage 2 he drew concerning the predictive-inductive inference. That is, that it is not 'reason', which 'engages' or 'determines' us to make inferences of that kind. What Hume means by saying this, will be determined later; but it is important to observe that it is what he concludes about the *a priori* and the predictive-inductive inference alike.

In the next section I will 'translate' some parts of Hume's terminology into language less likely to be misunderstood. It should be noticed, however, that even the version given above as the original contains one translation of sorts. This is the word 'presuppose', in premiss (e) of stage 2. Hume does not use this word. I have used it here not because its meaning is clear. On the contrary I think no word is used by philosophers with more ambiguity, and it will be part of our task in the next section to attach to it just one of its several possible meanings. I have used it because it is the obvious choice of one word which is to stand for a rather remarkable variety of phrases, all equally unclear, which Hume employs when he is stating his premiss (e).[14]

---

[14] In the following quotations I have italicized the phrase which was silently translated above as 'presuppose'.

'... all reasonings from experience *are founded on the supposition* that the course of nature will continue uniformly the same' (*Abstract*, p. 293).

'All probable arguments *are built on the supposition* that there is this conformity betwixt the future and the past...' (*Abstract*, p. 294).

'... probability *is founded on the presumption of* a resemblance betwixt those objects, of which we have had experience (etc.)' (*Treatise*, p. 90).

'... all our experimental conclusions *proceed upon the supposition* that the future will be conformable to the past.' (*Enquiry*, p. 35).

'... all inferences from experience *suppose, as their foundation*, that the future will resemble the past.' (*Enquiry*, p. 37).

(iii) Some translations of Hume's terminology

In stage 1 of Hume's argument there is only one matter which calls for clarification. This is, what Hume means when he says, in the conclusion (d), that the *a priori* inference is not one which 'reason' 'engages' us to make.

But this question, as we know, arises equally in connection with the conclusion (j) of stage 2, since Hume there says the very same thing about the predictive-inductive inference. We can therefore at the same time deal with one query concerning stage 2, and the only one which arises concerning stage 1. What, then, did Hume mean by saying, of a certain kind of inference, that it is not 'reason' (or 'reasoning', or 'our reason') which 'engages' (or 'determines') us to make it?

The answer I will give here to this question will be one which I do not offer as final, for in Chapter 4 below I intend to offer a much more specific answer to it.

The reason why (j) and (d) require at least some translation at present is that they appear on the surface to be propositions of a kind which it is certain they really are not. Hume's two conclusions appear to be factual, and in particular, psychological propositions: as though (j), for example, were Hume's answer to a causal question, 'What faculty of the mind is it which is at work in us when we make predictive-inductive inferences?' But to any philosophical reader of Hume it will be obvious that this appearance is misleading. Here, at any rate, Hume's interest in the inferences he discusses is not empirical and psychological, but rather the kind of interest which a philosopher usually takes in inferences: viz. an evaluative, and in some sense, logico-philosophical interest. In the conclusions (j) and (d) as they stand, we have in fact just another instance of what we know to be true in general of Hume (as of most philosophers between the seventeenth and twentieth centuries): that he asserts logico-philosophical theses in the guise of remarks about the constitution of the human mind.

Instead of an apparently psychological proposition, therefore, (j) should be rendered as a proposition evaluative, in some sense, of a certain class of inferences (viz. predictive-inductive ones). Not just any evaluation would do, of course. For there can be no doubt that Hume intends by (j) an extremely unfavourable evaluation of the inferences which are its subject. After all, (j) *is* that famous sceptical conclusion which Hume came to about inductive inferences, or rather, about the only 'species' of inductive inference which he discussed both clearly and at length. (If (j) is *not* Hume's inductive scepticism, there is no inductive scepticism anywhere in Hume).

I therefore suggest, as the interim translation of (j): 'All predictive-inductive inferences are unreasonable.' This captures the non-psychological, the evaluative, and the unfavourable meaning of Hume's conclusion in stage 2. The predicate 'unreasonable', indeed, cries out for further explanation, and this will be given in Chapter 4. In the meantime we must, accordingly, translate (d) as: 'All *a priori* inferences are unreasonable.'

Hume himself, it is worthy of notice, does not always express his two conclusions in such a way as to give them a misleading psychological appearance, and when he does not, his language comes very close to that which we have just adopted for (j) and (d). Consider, for example, the passage from the *Treatise*,[15] and especially the phrases I have italicized, in which he summarizes the conclusions of both stages of his argument, as follows: 'That there is nothing in any object, consider'd in itself, which can afford us *a reason* for drawing a conclusion beyond it; and, That even after the observation of the . . . constant conjunction of objects, we have *no reason* to draw any inference concerning any object beyond those of which we have had experience . . .' The conclusion (d) here is of course the part of this quotation before the semi-colon; the part after it is (j). Both parts are italicized in the original, and the passage shows other signs, as well, of having been written with special care. The result is, as we see, that Hume's conclusions, even though they still refer to 'reason', have been quite shorn of their usual pseudo-psychological air, and stand forth clearly in the character which my translations ascribe to them, of (adverse) evaluative propositions about certain classes of inferences.

I now turn to the premisses and intermediate steps of stage 2 of Hume's argument, to consider the meaning of certain words and phrases occurring there.

In premiss (f) of stage 2 Hume says, of the proposition that unobserved instances will resemble observed ones, that it concerns 'matter of fact and existence'. This is not a phrase which a present-day philosopher would be likely to employ, but a general acquaintance with Hume's philosophical terminology leaves no difficulty in translating it. Hume means by it, that the proposition in question is a contingent one.

[15] p. 139.

The translation of Hume's 'demonstrative', as applied to arguments in (g), presents hardly any more real difficulty. Yet it is here that the danger of misunderstanding his argument begins to become serious.

Here as elsewhere Hume meant by a 'demonstrative argument', a '(valid) argument *from necessarily true premisses*'. This is the only sense of the phrase which would explain Hume's own argument from (f) to (g); for it will be seen that the only ground which Hume gives for saying that there can be no demonstrative arguments for the Resemblance Thesis (as I will call it), is that that thesis is a *contingent* proposition. It is also the only sense of the phrase which is consistent with Hume's many variations on the theme that there can be no demonstrative arguments for any conclusion concerning matter of fact.[16]

Using 'demonstrative' of arguments in this sense was not, of course, on Hume's part, idiosyncratic in the slightest degree. This sense of the word is now somewhat obsolete, but by no means altogether so. It lingers on in the application to mathematics and logic of the title of 'demonstrative' sciences; for we still mean to convey by this, at least that the reasoning employed in those sciences is always from non-contingent premisses.

For the most part, however, it is not in this sense that philosophers nowadays apply the word 'demonstrative' to arguments or inferences. We almost always mean by it, especially if we use it as Hume so often does, in opposition to 'probable arguments', just that the arguments in question are valid. Our sense of 'demonstrative argument', then, is purely evaluative, and quite independent of the kind of premisses the argument has. (Our sense of 'probable', applied to an argument, is similarly purely evaluative: we mean by it just that the argument in question has a high, though not the highest possible, degree of conclusiveness.) But to suppose that Hume used 'demonstrative argument' in this sense would be to impute to him an error unbelievably gross and often repeated. For he would then be saying, each time he asserts that there can be no

[16] For example: '... wherever a demonstration takes place the contrary is impossible and implies a contradiction' (*Abstract*, p. 293). 'What is possible can never be demonstrated to be false...' (*Abstract*, p. 294). 'Were a proposition demonstratively false, it would imply a contradiction...' (*Enquiry*, p. 26). '... Whatever is intelligible... implies no contradiction, and can never be proved false by any demonstrative argument or abstract reasoning *a priori*' (*Enquiry*, p. 35). '... the only objects of the abstract science or of demonstration are quantity and number...' (*Enquiry*, p. 163).

demonstrative arguments for a matter of fact, that there cannot be a valid argument which has a contingent conclusion!

The position is very similar (*mutatis mutandis*) with regard to Hume's use, in (e), (h), and (i), of the word 'probable', applied to arguments. Yet it is in connection with this word that the danger of misunderstanding Hume's argument is at its greatest. What, then, does Hume mean here by 'probable arguments'? And by the word which (cf. e.g. note 14 above) he uses interchangeably with 'probable arguments', 'probability'?

This question is of fundamental importance for everything which follows in this book, and although it is not really at all difficult to answer, special care is therefore required here. The safest way to proceed will be by breaking this question up into two separate questions, each of which is extremely easy to answer, and of which the answers together will give us the answer to the above question.

I ask first, therefore, a different question: what is the main topic of Book I Part III of the *Treatise*, of the *Abstract*, and of sections iv–vi of the *Enquiry*? As a first approximation, the answer could hardly be more obvious. The main topic of these parts of Hume's writings is certain kinds of inference. For one of Hume's purposes obviously was to evaluate those inferences. But even in order to state what Hume's evaluative conclusions were, it must be possible for us to refer, in a neutral, non-evaluative way, to the class of inferences which were the subject of his evaluations. What inferences, then, are the main subject of these parts of Hume's writings?

It will be safest to proceed here by a series of approximations. First, then (just as for Hume a 'demonstrative argument' is one from necessary premisses), the arguments which are his main topic in Book I Part III of the *Treatise* etc., are, evidently, arguments from *contingent* premisses. Thus he sometimes writes, in the course of stating (h), that arguments for the Resemblance Thesis must be 'probable only, *or such as regard matter of fact and real existence*'.[17] Again, in stating (i), he sometimes speaks of 'probable arguments, *or arguments regarding existence*'.[18] Similarly, Hume sometimes uses the phrase 'moral evidence'[19] as a name for the kind of inference which he is discussing; and whatever more that may mean, it surely at least means 'arguments from contingent premisses'. So far,

---

[17] *Enquiry*, p. 35. My italics.
[18] Ibid. pp. 35–6. My italics.
[19] Ibid. p. 35, and again p. 158.

then, Hume's topic can be characterized as being 'arguments from contingent premisses'.

Since, however, Hume cannot be supposed to have had in mind arguments from contingent premisses to non-contingent conclusions, we can safely add a further approximation. The arguments which were his subject-matter were arguments of which both the premiss and the conclusion are contingent.

The next restriction is also obvious. Hume's main topic was not at all 'arguments from and to contingent propositions' in general. It falls, rather, within the species of that genus in which the premisses of the arguments are not merely contingent but observational propositions: reports, that is, of actual or possible past or present experiences. His subject is 'arguments *from experience*',[20] 'reasonings *from experience*'.[21] This restriction, that the inferences under discussion are ones with observational premisses, is also part at least of what Hume means by his insistence that those inferences 'terminate'[22] in one or more *impressions*.

We have not yet characterized Hume's topic narrowly enough, however, for certainly it does not include every 'argument from observational premisses to a contingent conclusion'. The latter class includes the kind of inference which in section (*i*) above was called the *a priori* inference (for example, from 'This is a flame' to 'This is hot'). It also includes, for example, the inference from 'This is an orange flame' to 'This is a flame'. But the inferences which are the main subject-matter of the *Treatise* Book I Part III, etc., are certainly very different ones from either of these.

The class of inferences we are seeking is, of course, just that proper sub-class of arguments from observational premisses to contingent conclusions, of which the predictive-inductive inference is a typical, and the most important, member. The next most important member of the class, according to Hume, is the kind of inference which he discusses in section xii of Book I Part III of the *Treatise* (and in the corresponding fourth paragraph of section vi of the *Enquiry*). This is the class of inference of which the following example, based again on one of Hume's, will serve us as a paradigm: 'Nearly all of the many ships observed leaving port in the past have returned safely, and this is a ship leaving port, so, this will return safely.'

---

[20] Ibid. p. 38 and p. 56 footnote, for example. My italics.
[21] *Abstract*, p. 293. My italics.   [22] *Enquiry*, p. 46; cf. *Treatise*, p. 89.

Since its typical and most important members are the predictive-inductive inference and the similar ('ship') inference from frequent conjunction, the class of inferences in question can be further characterized as being 'arguments from observed to unobserved instances of empirical predicates'. Or, more simply, and finally, as 'inductive arguments'.

These characterizations are, of course, like all the earlier approximations to them, entirely non-evaluative of the class of inferences which they pick out. For we have been trying precisely to determine what inferences were the subject of Hume's evaluative conclusions.

That the main topic of Book I Part III of the *Treatise*, of the *Abstract*, and of sections iv–vi of the *Enquiry* is what we call inductive inferences, is obvious enough; and it was in fact taken for granted in section (*i*) of this chapter. But it was worthwhile to labour to establish the obvious here, because to do so takes us so far towards answering the vital question on which we are engaged, of what Hume meant by 'probable arguments' in the argument diagrammed above.

Let us ask, then, the second easy question which now will enable us to answer the question just mentioned. What word or phrase did Hume use to refer, in a non-evaluative way, to the inferences which it was at least one of his objects to evaluate? Not, of course, 'inductive inference'; and in fact, as was remarked earlier, Hume uses a variety of phrases for this purpose—'arguments concerning existence', 'arguments from experience', 'moral evidence', etc. But there is one word and one phrase which every reader of Hume will easily recognize as his favourite synonyms for each of these phrases and for our 'inductive inference'. They are 'probability' and 'probable arguments'.

The whole of Book I Part III of the *Treatise*, for example, is 'Of Knowledge and Probability', and apart from section i 'Of knowledge', all of that part, beginning with section ii 'Of probability; and of the idea of cause and effect', has for its main topic what Hume calls 'probability' or 'probable arguments'. Its main topic, however, is also what we call 'inductive inferences'. Therefore what Hume means by 'probable arguments', in (e), (h), and (i) of the argument diagrammed above, is simply 'inductive inferences'.

Although the textual support for it seems, and I think is, irresistible, this translation is sure to cause some demur, and it is not hard to see why. Our sense of 'probable arguments' is evaluative, and even purely so. We use 'probable' of an argument to mean 'of high but not the highest possible degree of conclusiveness'. Yet according to the above translation, Hume used 'probable arguments' in a purely non-evaluative sense. It would be difficult to believe that between his time and ours the word 'probable' has acquired its evaluative meaning for the first time. But could Hume have been so insensitive to the element of evaluation in the meaning of the word 'probable' as my translation requires him to have been?

Indeed he could have been. For it is in fact possible to prove decisively that he was a great deal more insensitive to the normal evaluative meaning of the words which he chose to use as non-evaluative names for certain classes of inferences than my translation of 'probable' as 'inductive' represents him as being.

At the outset of section xi of the *Treatise* Book I Part III, and of the corresponding section vi of the *Enquiry*, Hume announces a change in his sense of 'probability' and 'probable arguments': a change which narrows the range of application of those words.

At this stage of the *Treatise* and *Enquiry*, of course, the discussion of the predictive-inductive inference, and hence the argument which is diagrammed above, is over. Hume is about to turn his attention to 'some other species of reasoning', of which the main one is the inference from frequent conjunction (the inference about the ships). In the *Treatise* he opens this group of three sections, xi–xiii, with the following interesting paragraphs.

But in order to bestow on this system its full force and evidence, we must carry our eye from it a moment to consider its consequences, and explain from the same principles some other species of reasoning, which are deriv'd from the same origin.

Those philosophers, who have divided human reason into *knowledge and probability*, and have defin'd the first to be *that evidence, which arises from the comparison of ideas*, are obliged to comprehend all our arguments from causes or effects under the general term of probability. But tho' every one be free to use his terms in what sense he pleases; and accordingly in the precedent parts of this discourse, I have follow'd this method of expression; 'tis however certain, that in common discourse we readily affirm, that many arguments from causation exceed probability, and may be receiv'd as a superior kind of evidence. One wou'd appear ridiculous, who wou'd say, that 'tis only probable the sun will rise tomorrow, or that all men must dye; tho' 'tis plain we have no further assurance of these facts, than what experience affords us. For this reason, 'twould perhaps be more convenient, in order at once to preserve the common signification of words, and mark the several degrees of evidence, to distinguish human reason into three kinds, viz. *that from knowledge, from proofs, and from probabilities*. By knowledge, I mean the assurance arising from the comparison of ideas. By proofs, those arguments which are derived from the relation of cause and effect, and which are entirely free from doubt and uncertainty. By probability, that evidence, which is still attended with uncertainty. 'Tis this last species of reasoning, I proceed to examine.[23]

The section 'Of Probability' in the *Enquiry*, which is what corresponds to sections xi–xiii of the *Treatise*, opens with a precisely parallel explanation.[24]

Thus, 'in the precedent parts of this discourse', and hence in the sections which contain the argument diagrammed above, Hume had used 'probability' to 'comprehend all our arguments from causes or effects', or all 'arguments from experience' as he calls them in the corresponding *Enquiry* passage. Now, however (that is, for sections xi–xiii in the *Treatise*, and section vi in the *Enquiry*), he proposes to confine 'probability' and 'probable arguments' just to such of those arguments as are 'attended with uncertainty'. For the predictive-inductive inference, which is not so 'attended', he now adopts the name 'proof'.

This passage provides additional evidence that Hume had used 'probable arguments' quite non-evaluatively in the earlier sections. For the *differentia* which he gives of the kinds of inferences to be discussed in sections xi–xiii is not at all evaluative. A kind of inference's being 'attended with uncertainty' is simply a matter of how it *is* evaluated *in fact and by men*. Hume is, once again, giving an evaluatively neutral name to some inferences which it is no doubt part of his intention to go on to evaluate. But if the new, narrower sense of 'probability'—in effect, 'inductive inferences generally recognized as uncertain'—is non-evaluative, as it is, then *a fortiori* the earlier, wider sense of 'probability', viz. 'inductive inferences', is also non-evaluative.

But the most striking thing about the passage quoted above is the application which Hume proposes in it for the word 'proof'. Now the word 'proof', both in Hume's time and ours, is one which when applied to inferences or arguments, is not only evaluative but in the highest degree expressive of favourable evaluation. Yet the class of inferences on which Hume now bestows this name is none other

[23] *Treatise*, p. 124. Hume's italics.
[24] *Enquiry*, p. 56, footnote appended to the title of the section.

than that of predictive-inductive inferences. That is, precisely those inferences which he has just before been at great pains to reach an extremely unfavourable evaluative conclusion about! No one who had just argued for the conclusion (j) of stage 2 of Hume's argument, about the predictive-inductive inference, could possibly go on to call that kind of inference 'proof', unless he were insensitive to the normal evaluative meaning of the word 'proof'. There is therefore no difficulty whatever in supposing that *a fortiori* Hume's use of 'probable arguments' was, what my translation made it, entirely non-evaluative.

Hume's choice of names for various classes of arguments, it must be admitted, was not well-advised. Since in the *Enquiry*, and in the *Treatise* Book I Part III, his main object evidently was to evaluate, in some sense, various kinds of arguments from experience, he should have first introduced those arguments under clearly non-evaluative names. To introduce them under names already in use with an evaluative meaning was bound to involve him either in the appearance of begging the very question he wished to ask, or in the appearance of self-contradiction; according as the evaluation which he arrived at, of a certain argument, was or was not the same as the evaluation implicit in the name he used for it. Since in the case of most of the 'species of reasoning' which he discussed, Hume's evaluation was *not* the same as that which his name for it conveys, what he says often has the appearance of self-contradiction; as when he calls arguments, of which his own evaluation is unfavourable in the extreme, 'probable' arguments, and even 'proofs'.

Still, this defect is really only name-deep, as it were. On the whole Hume could have hardly done more than he did to make clear to his readers that his senses of 'probable arguments' (both the wide and the narrow sense), and his various names for special kinds of inductive inference, were all of them entirely non-evaluative.

The word 'inductive' was applied to arguments, in the foregoing paragraphs, in what I believe to be the sense which it has customarily had: that of 'arguments from observed to unobserved instances of empirical predicates'. This is also the sense in which it will be used throughout the remainder of this book. But it deserves to be emphasized that, in consequence, the word 'inductive' here has no evaluative meaning whatever. In particular, it is not and will never be part of what I mean by calling an inference 'inductive' that that inference has less than the highest possible degree of conclusiveness.

Many contemporary readers will probably find some difficulty in resisting the temptation to read this element into the meaning of 'inductive'. Why this is so, and why the temptation should nevertheless be resisted, will appear from Chapters 3, 7, and 8 below. The temptation would not be avoided, but would if anything be strengthened, if I were to adhere, for a translation of Hume's 'probable arguments', to the phrase 'arguments from observed to unobserved instances of empirical predicates'. The fact is, as we shall see, that Hume's influence on the history of thought has set us here a problem of nomenclature which has no completely satisfactory solution. The best way for the reader (at least if the experience of the writer is any guide) to avoid importing an evaluative element into my 'inductive' or Hume's 'probable arguments', is for him to keep in the forefront of his mind just the concrete paradigms which have been introduced of this class of arguments; principally, of course, the predictive-inductive inference about the flames.

The last problem of translation concerns the word 'presuppose' in premiss (e) of Hume's argument. What did Hume mean by saying that probable arguments *presuppose* that unobserved instances of empirical predicates resemble observed ones? (Or rather, since 'presuppose' was my own word, what did he mean by the variety of phrases, listed in note 14 above, for which 'presuppose' was an apt, though unilluminating, paraphrase?) In what sense is it true that predictive-inductive inferences, for example, presuppose that unobserved instances resemble observed ones?

The senses in which an argument can 'presuppose' a proposition are many, and they are not often enough distinguished by philosophers. One such sense is this. An argument from premiss p to conclusion q is sometimes said to presuppose a proposition r, in the sense that unless r were *true*, no one could be in a position to acquire belief in the premiss p. In this sense, the predictive-inductive inference about the flames, for example, presupposes, among other things, that there is such a property as heat.

It is not in this sense of the word, however, that 'presuppose' occurs in premiss (e). For in this sense (e) is obviously false; or at any rate would certainly have been thought false by Hume. The last thing he would have wished to maintain is that no one could be in a position to acquire belief in 'This is a flame and all of the many flames observed in the past have been hot', unless future flames *do* resemble past ones! Some of Hume's more optimistic critics appear to believe that something like this is indeed true; but that is an additional reason, if any were needed, for thinking that it is not the above sense of 'presuppose' that Hume intends in the premiss (e).

I cannot hope to show, of every sense of 'presuppose' except the one I will adopt, that it could not have been Hume's. I must instead proceed directly, and state what I think *is* Hume's sense of the word. This cannot fail to introduce an element of uncertainty into my account of his argument. But I will be able to show that the risk of error involved is very small.

Sometimes when we say of an argument from p to q, that it presupposes r, our meaning is as follows: that, as it stands, the argument from p to q is not valid, and that, in order to turn it into a valid argument, it would be necessary to add to its premisses the proposition r. I believe that this is the sense in which 'presuppose' occurs in premiss (e) of Hume's argument.

My grounds for this belief are two. The first is that when 'presuppose' is taken in this sense (and 'probable arguments' is translated as 'inductive arguments', in the sense stated above), (e) comes out true. For (e) would then say this: 'Inductive arguments are all invalid as they stand, and it would be necessary, in order to turn them into valid arguments, to add to their premisses a proposition which asserts that unobserved instances resemble observed ones.' And so interpreted, (e) is true. Consider a typical inductive argument, such as the predictive-inductive inference from 'This is a flame, and all of the many flames observed in the past have been hot' to 'This is hot.' It is invalid as it stands. Nor could it be turned into a valid argument without the addition of some further premiss which will have the effect of saying that (at least in respect of heat) flames yet unobserved resemble observed flames. This additional premiss could take many non-equivalent forms. Perhaps the weakest of all of them would be the conditional proposition, 'If this is a flame and all of the many flames observed in the past have been hot then this is hot.' But the addition, to the original premiss, of *some* Resemblance Thesis is clearly needed if this typical inductive argument is to be turned into a valid one.

My second ground for thinking that in (e) 'presuppose' means what I have suggested, is that when it is taken in this sense (and 'probable' is translated as 'inductive'), the conclusion which Hume drew from (e) combined with (h) is perfectly explained. For (e)

44 *Its structure and content*

would, again, say this: 'Inductive arguments are all invalid as they stand, and it would be necessary, in order to turn them into valid arguments, to add to their premisses the Resemblance Thesis.' The translation of (h) is: 'Any arguments for the Resemblance Thesis must be inductive ones.' Together these two propositions entail that any inductive arguments for the Resemblance Thesis would be such that they could be turned into valid ones only by the addition to their premisses of the Resemblance Thesis itself; only, that is, by having their conclusion as a premiss, or in other words, by being circular. But that is precisely what the proposition (i), which is inferred by Hume from the conjunction of (e) and (h), says.

Now, it is very unlikely that any suggested sense of 'presuppose', if it were not the one that Hume intended, would both make his premiss (e) true, and so neatly explain the inference Hume made from (e), with (h), to (i). I do not know of any sense of 'presuppose', other than the one I have advanced, which fulfils even one of these two desiderata. Consequently there can be little risk of error in supposing that Hume did mean by 'presuppose' in (e) what I have suggested he meant.

(iv) The argument after these translations have been made

For ease of reference it will be best if I now bring all my translations together, and state what I take the whole of Hume's argument to have been.

The structure of the argument is of course not changed. It remains as in the diagram:

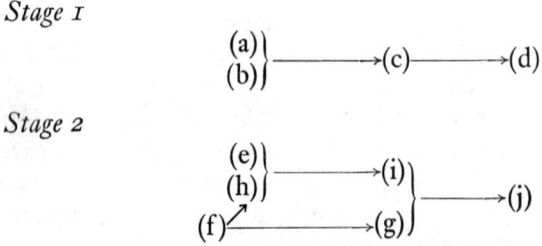

But the content of the argument, incorporating both my abbreviations ('*a priori* inference', 'predictive-inductive inference', and 'Resemblance Thesis'), and my various translations, is now as follows.

Dictionary

Stage 1

(a) Whatever is intelligible, is possible.

(b) All *a priori* inferences are such that the supposition, that the premiss is true and the conclusion false, is intelligible.

(c) That supposition is always possible.

(d) All *a priori* inferences are unreasonable.

Stage 2

(e) All inductive arguments are invalid as they stand, and are such that, in order to turn them into valid arguments, it is necessary to add the Resemblance Thesis to their premisses.

(f) The Resemblance Thesis is a contingent proposition.

(g) The Resemblance Thesis cannot be validly inferred from necessarily true premisses.

(h) Any arguments for the Resemblance Thesis must be inductive ones.

(i) Any inductive argument for the Resemblance Thesis would be circular.

(j) All predictive-inductive inferences are unreasonable.

3

ITS SUPPRESSED PREMISSES

(i) One suppressed premiss

If there is anything about this argument of Hume which is more admirable than its content, it is the explicitness of it. Almost always, the main obstacle to the evaluation of an argument, and often an insuperable obstacle, is the difficulty of identifying it—of finding out what the argument actually is. How seldom when men argue, in philosophy or elsewhere, can one confidently draw up the structure-diagram and dictionary of their arguments! In the case of Hume's argument for predictive-inductive scepticism, however, one can do so. One can even, as we have seen, substitute for Hume's phraseology at the places where it could nowadays be misleading, other phrases which one can be confident express his meaning.

Admirably explicit as it is, Hume's argument is yet not entirely explicit. Philosophers almost always (even if they happen to be discussing invalid arguments), intend their own arguments to be valid ones, and in this respect Hume was no exception. He certainly was not advancing, for his sceptical conclusion about certain 'probable arguments' in his sense, an argument which he regarded as merely a probable one in *our* sense; that is, an argument of less than the highest possible degree of conclusiveness! Yet it is obvious that his argument is not valid as it stands, either in stage 1 or stage 2. Hume has suppressed, as being too obvious to require expression, certain propositions which are nevertheless necessary for the validity of his argument. One of these will be pointed out in the next paragraph, and a second, less obvious one, in section *(iii)* below.

In stage 2, Hume appears to infer (g), 'The Resemblance Thesis cannot be validly inferred from necessarily true premisses', from (f) alone; i.e. from 'The Resemblance Thesis is a contingent proposition'. But if a man, intending his argument to be valid, infers the former proposition apparently solely from the latter, we are entitled

One suppressed premiss 47

to conclude that his stated premiss is not really his only one. He must be assuming, in addition, that *no contingent proposition can be validly inferred from necessarily true premisses*. This proposition, therefore, is a suppressed premiss which we must ascribe to Hume's argument for predictive-inductive scepticism. It may be alternatively but equivalently phrased as: 'All arguments from necessarily true premisses to contingent conclusions are invalid.' In the language of Hume, of course, this suppressed premiss would be, 'There can be no demonstrative arguments for a matter of fact': a proposition which we know (cf. note 16, Chapter 2 above) that Hume not only believed, but often asserted.

(ii) What follows from the premisses mentioned so far

For the conclusion (j), then, Hume's argument has just three premisses which we have noticed so far: the two premisses he stated, (e) and (f), and the unstated one just mentioned. It will prove profitable to ask at this point, how far these premisses, unaided by any other assumptions, go towards establishing the sceptical conclusion which Hume drew (that predictive-inductive inferences are unreasonable). What is the *most* that these premisses entail about the predictive-inductive inference?

I do not know of any mechanical way of answering this question, but intuitively it is not difficult to answer. What (e), (f), and the first suppressed premiss really do entail about predictive-inductive inferences, but also all that they entail, is the following proposition. 'All predictive-inductive inferences are invalid as they stand; and in order to turn them into valid inferences, it is necessary to add to their premisses a proposition which cannot be validly inferred from necessarily true premisses, and which cannot be validly inferred, either, from observational premisses, without such an addition to them as would make that inference circular.'

This is a proposition of considerable complexity. Fortunately it is possible to reduce it to much more manageable proportions, if we break it up into its three natural clauses, and consider each of these in turn.

It can hardly be supposed that the phrase, 'as they stand', adds anything to the content of the first clause. That clause, therefore, reduces simply to 'All predictive-inductive inferences are invalid'.

Now, given this, the second clause above is redundant, and can simply be omitted. For a proposition can be validly inferred from necessary truths if and only if it is itself a necessary truth. Thus the second clause merely says that the addition to their premisses which is necessary to turn predictive-inductive inferences into valid ones, is not a necessary truth. But this follows from their being invalid inferences (to contingent conclusions) in the first place.

Now as to the third clause. What can be validly inferred from observational premisses, without such an addition to them as would make an inference to the Resemblance Thesis circular, is just what can be validly inferred from observational premisses alone. Now every proposition which can be validly inferred from observational premisses alone is itself either an observation-statement or a necessary truth; and every observation-statement or necessary truth can be validly inferred from observational premisses alone. Consequently, the third clause of the proposition above merely says that the proposition which needs to be added to the premisses of predictive-inductive inferences in order to make them valid, is not either an observation-statement or a necessary truth. The second disjunct here is redundant, and can simply be omitted, for the same reason that the whole of the second clause was. Then the third clause just says that the additional premiss needed to make predictive-inductive inferences valid is not observational. Or contrapositively, that the addition of any observational premiss to a predictive-inductive inference is insufficient to make it valid.

Thus the whole proposition stated above reduces to this: that all predictive-inductive inferences are invalid, and that all the inferences, which result from supplementing the premisses of a predictive-inductive inference by further observational premisses, are also invalid.

This proposition, as distinct from Hume's scepticism (j), which says that predictive-inductive inferences are all unreasonable, I will refer to as Hume's predictive-inductive 'fallibilism'. For it is only a judgement of invalidity, though of course a very general one. It says, of the predictive-inductive inference and certain others, no more than that it is possible for them to have true premisses and false conclusions. And since this proposition really does follow from Hume's premisses, (e), (f), and the suppressed premiss noticed in the preceding section, I will sometimes refer to it as the fallibilist *consequence*, as distinct from the sceptical *conclusion* (j), of his argument.

The thesis of predictive-inductive fallibilism will perhaps appear trivial. It is sure to appear so, and indeed to be so, if the reader, forgetting that 'inductive' is being used here in a purely descriptive sense, were to take as part of the meaning of calling an argument 'inductive', that that argument is invalid. In fact, however, as will be shown in Chapters 7 and 8 below, the fallibilist thesis is very far from being trivial.

At any rate it is, I affirm, *the most* that follows about the predictive-inductive inference from Hume's stated premisses, in conjunction with the unstated one noticed above.

(iii) A second suppressed premiss

This claim meets with some interesting confirmations from Hume himself. For occasionally he writes as though his conclusion were only the fallibilist one. For example, when he represents his conclusion as being just that 'nothing leads us to this inference [i.e. the predictive-inductive inference] but custom or a certain instinct of our nature; which it is indeed difficult to resist, but which, like other instincts, *may be fallacious and deceitful*'.[1] On another occasion he writes similarly, of the 'Sceptick', that 'all he means . . . is to abate the pride of mere human reasoners, by showing them, that even with regard to principles which seem the clearest, and which they are necessitated from the strongest instincts of nature to embrace, *they are not able to obtain a full consistence and absolute certainty*'.[2]

The second of these quotations can weigh very little with us, when we recall the occasion of the pamphlet from which it is taken. For the *Letter from a Gentleman* was of course a desperate attempt by Hume to prevent public criticism of the 'scepticism' of the *Treatise* from prejudicing his candidature for a chair at Edinburgh University. In such passages, in fact, as is admitted even by the most sympathetic of Hume's biographers and editors (Professor Mossner), the pamphlet is not easily freed from the suspicion of being actually 'disingenuous'.[3]

[1] *Enquiry*, p. 159. My italics.
[2] *A Letter from a Gentleman to his Friend in Edinburgh* (ed. Mossner and Price, Edinburgh, 1967), p. 19 of the facsimile of Hume's pamphlet of 1745. My italics. This pamphlet swarms with printing errors, and the general sense of the passage quoted suggests that the printer may have mistaken the word 'confidence' in Hume's handwriting for 'consistence'. The calligraphy of 1745 would have made just such a mistake especially easy.
[3] Ibid., p. xxiv of the editors' introduction.

Nor can occasional fallibilist versions of Hume's conclusion, such as the first passage quoted above, count for much. For they have to be set against all of the many passages in which Hume expresses his conclusion as being that knowledge of the premises of a predictive-inductive inference gives us (not just a logically insufficient reason but) *no* reason, no more reason than we had prior to all experience, for believing the conclusion.

The conclusion, then, which Hume drew in stage 2, is rightly represented as being the sceptical one, that all predictive-inductive inferences are unreasonable. If what was said in the preceding section was correct, however, the most that follows about predictive-inductive inferences from the premises which we have so far ascribed to Hume, is the fallibilist consequence, that predictive-inductive inference are all invalid. Now the former proposition certainly does not follow from the latter. Hume, however, as has been said earlier in this chapter, undoubtedly intended his argument to be a valid one. We must, therefore, ascribe to Hume the additional premiss which is needed to make this inference, from predictive-inductive fallibilism to predictive-inductive scepticism, valid. That is the thesis that *all invalid arguments are unreasonable*. I will refer to this, for obvious reasons, as the thesis of 'deductivism'. It is the second suppressed premiss which is needed to make Hume's argument to his sceptical conclusion valid.

Most fortunately, it is possible to verify independently the necessity of ascribing this thesis to Hume. For consider stage 1 of his argument. Here Hume draws, concerning the *a priori* inference, the same conclusion in (d) as he draws later in (j) concerning the predictive-inductive inference, viz. that it is unreasonable. But the only stated premises of stage 1, viz. (a) and (b), clearly entail no more than this, that all *a priori* inferences are such that it is possible for them to have true premises and false conclusions; that is, that they are all invalid. Yet Hume certainly concluded that they are unreasonable. He must, therefore, have assumed in stage 1 of his argument, as well as in stage 2, though he did not state, that all invalid inferences are unreasonable. (My attribution to Hume of deductivism as a suppressed premiss in stage 2 rested on my reduction of the fallibilist consequence to manageable proportions. Consequently the present discovery of deductivism as a suppressed premiss elsewhere in his argument constitutes a confirmation of the correctness of that reduction.)

(*iv*) *The essence of Hume's argument*

Hume's argument in stage 2 may therefore be summed up in the following way: from premisses which prove at most the invalidity of predictive-inductive inferences, along with the unstated premiss that an inference is unreasonable if it is invalid, Hume concluded that predictive-inductive inferences are unreasonable.

It is, of course, only in its detail that this account of Hume's argument differs from that which has been given by many other writers. That the conclusion Hume drew about inductive inferences was a *sceptical* one; that he had a 'rationalistic' (i.e. deductivist) conception of what inferences 'reason' can sanction; and that his great positive contribution was a certain thesis of non-deducibility (i.e. invalidity)—these three things may be said to be nearly common property among philosophers.[4] Vague as they are, each of them is

---

[4] (Footnote added in June 1972.) Much more than this, however, is common to the account which up to this point I have given of Hume's argument and an account of it which was given by the late Professor Dickinson S. Miller in an article in *The Journal of Philosophy*, vol. 46, 1949, esp. p. 745. For the essence of Hume's argument is there represented as being from (what I call) inductive fallibilism to inductive scepticism via the suppressed premiss that 'all rational inference is deductive'; which premiss the author even calls the thesis of 'deductivism'!

Between Miller's treatment and mine there is, indeed, this important difference, that I believed it necessary to *justify* the attribution of the above argument to Hume, whereas Miller apparently did not. Accordingly I have here devoted two whole chapters of a basically textual nature to this end, whereas Miller devotes not one word. He does not, in support of his attribution of the argument to Hume, refer even once to Hume's text. He simply makes the attribution, in the first few lines of his article, and then plunges straight into the philosophy of the matter.

Nevertheless, between the argument which Miller attributed to Hume, and the argument I attribute to Hume, the similarity is strikingly complete: so complete, indeed, that it cannot be unnecessary for me to state that I arrived at my account independently of Miller's. In fact I read Miller's article for the first time on 6 June 1972; more than a year, that is, after finishing the text of this book, and more than two years after publishing (in my article 'Deductivism', *Australasian Journal of Philosophy*, vol. 48, May 1970) an account of Hume's argument which is in most respects the same as I have given here.

In the discussion (published and unpublished) which followed the article of mine just referred to, no one pointed out its similarity to the starting-point of Miller's article. This now seems surprising, but the explanation must be, I think, that his article had been overlooked, however undeservedly, not only by me but by almost everyone else. I cannot remember ever having seen, before I read it, a reference to it in a philosophical journal. I learnt of its existence only from the valuable compilation by Roland Hall, 'A Hume Bibliography' (York, 1971).

That my account of Hume's argument should be essentially the same as that arrived at independently by another philosopher is some additional reason for thinking it a true account. But there is also a second respect in which Miller's article is confirmatory of propositions I had advanced. For it is entitled 'Hume's Deathblow to Deductivism', and according to Miller the philosophical value of Hume's argument lies in its being, not a

absolutely correct, if my account of Hume's argument is correct. Their wide currency, therefore, is some confirmation of the more detailed account of that argument which I have given.

_{proof of its sceptical conclusion, but an unintended *reductio ad absurdum* of its deductivist premiss. Now that is the very turn of thought in relation to Hume's argument, which I had said in Chapter 8 section (ii) of this book was characteristic of the first half of the present century. Miller's article (or rather its first page) is thus an especially striking, because unusually explicit, confirmation of what I said there.}

4

ITS FURTHER INTERPRETATION AND GENERALIZATION

(i) The nature of Hume's predictive-inductive scepticism: a statement of logical probability

What kind of proposition is Hume's sceptical conclusion (j), 'All predictive-inductive inferences are unreasonable'? The same kind, at any rate, as his earlier conclusion (d), 'All *a priori* inferences are unreasonable.' I have argued, in Chapter 2 section (*iii*), that these two propositions are not psychological generalizations, but rather propositions evaluative, in some sense, of the two classes of inferences which are their respective subjects. In the present section my first object is to prove a more general result, that they cannot be factual propositions of any kind whatever.

There *are*, indeed, it deserves to be noticed, two factual propositions about the *a priori* and the predictive-inductive inference respectively, which Hume does repeatedly assert and imply. These propositions concern the degrees of belief which a knowledge of the premisses of the two inferences actually produces in the minds of men. These degrees of belief are, of course, according to Hume, very different in the two cases. Knowledge of 'This is a flame', the premiss of the *a priori* inference, is not sufficient, as a matter of fact, to produce in us any belief whatever in the conclusion 'This is hot.' The first flame we observe is no more effective, in leading us to anticipate heat, than is a complete absence of experience. Experience of the conjunction, in all of many instances, of heat with flame is necessary to make us believe, when we observe a further flame, that it will be hot.[1] Such experience once acquired, however, is sufficient, as well as necessary, to produce such belief; and it even produces, according to Hume, 'the last degree of assurance'[2] in the truth of

---
[1] See, for example, *Abstract*, p. 293; *Enquiry*, p. 42; *Treatise*, p. 87.
[2] *Enquiry*, p. 110.

the conclusion 'This is hot.' (The predictive-inductive inference, it will be recalled, was distinguished by Hume from 'probable arguments' in his *narrowed* sense, precisely and solely by its being, in practice and among men, 'entirely free from doubt and uncertainty'.)

Clearly, *these* propositions are factual and indeed psychological ones. They are propositions about how 'convincing'[3] the *a priori* and the predictive-inductive inferences respectively are in fact to men. Though they are not to be confused with (d) and (j), they will prove to be useful, by way of contrast, in determining the nature of those two conclusions.

What, then, *is* the nature of propositions (d) and (j)? Any answer to this question must be consistent with the following evident facts about those two propositions. (1) They are propositions about certain inferences. (2) They are universal propositions. Whatever it is that (j), for example, says about predictive-inductive inferences, it says about all inferences belonging to that class. (3) They are evaluations, of some kind, of the relevant classes of inferences. (4) They are *extremely adverse* evaluations, of the *a priori* and predictive-inductive inferences respectively.

These desiderata do not suffice to exclude a factual interpretation of (j) and (d). A proposition could perfectly well be an adverse evaluation of all predictive-inductive inferences, say, and still be a factual one. Suppose, for example, that by calling predictive-inductive inferences 'unreasonable', Hume had meant this: 'that every predictive-inductive inferrer will in fact almost always, in the long run, arrive at a false conclusion when his premisses are true'. This is a proposition which satisfies the four desiderata mentioned above for interpretations of (j); yet it is a factual proposition.

It is possible, however, to show with finality that (j) is not factual. But let us first show the same of the earlier conclusion (d). That conclusion, 'All *a priori* inferences are unreasonable', was as we have seen inferred by Hume from the three following premisses. (a) 'Whatever is intelligible is possible'; (b) 'All *a priori* inferences are such that the supposition, that the premiss is true and the conclusion false, is intelligible'; and the unstated deductivist premiss, 'All invalid arguments (i.e. arguments such that the truth of the premiss and falsity of the conclusion is possible) are unreasonable.' Now, the inference of Hume from these premisses to the conclusion (d)

[3] *Treatise*, p. 97 n.

The nature of Hume's scepticism

is a valid one. But not one of those three premisses is a proposition of a factual kind. Their conjunction, however (it will be assumed here, for the sake of Hume's argument), is consistent. Consequently the conclusion (d) which they entail cannot be a factual proposition either.

An exactly similar argument proves the non-factual character of (j). Hume's grounds for the conclusion, 'All predictive-inductive inferences are unreasonable', consist, as we have seen, of two stated and two unstated premisses. The stated ones were: (e) 'All inductive inferences are invalid, and are such that in order to turn them into valid inferences it is necessary to add the Resemblance Thesis to their premisses'; and (f) 'The Resemblance Thesis is contingent.' The unstated premisses were, first: 'All arguments from necessarily true premisses to contingent conclusions are invalid'; and second, the deductivist premiss, 'All invalid arguments are unreasonable.' Now, moreover, from these four premisses, the conclusion (j) which Hume drew from them really does follow. (For the first three suffice for fallibilism, which with deductivism suffices for scepticism.) But not one of those premisses is a proposition of a factual kind. Their conjunction, however (it will be assumed here, for the sake of Hume's argument), is consistent. Consequently the sceptical conclusion (j) 'All predictive-inductive inferences are unreasonable', which these premisses entail, cannot be a factual proposition either.

This is the most important result to which one is led by my identification of Hume's argument for (predictive-)inductive scepticism. It is the key to my evaluation of that argument in Part Three below. No evaluation, moreover, of Hume's argument is likely to be correct if it does not set out from the fact, ascertainable from the texts themselves, that his sceptical conclusion can be validly inferred, as it happens historically to have been inferred by Hume, from premisses which are exclusively non-factual. From premisses, to be specific, which consist of: two judgements of invalidity (viz. (e) and the first suppressed premiss); one attribution (f) of modal status to a certain proposition; and the premiss, which no one could mistake for a factual one, of deductivism.

There is another ground on which any factual interpretation of the conclusion (j) can be excluded. Although, as I have remarked earlier, Hume never expressly discussed the universal-inductive inference, he is always considered to have done so in effect, and to have known that he had done so, in the course of his discussion of the predictive-inductive inference. For it is very obvious, and certainly was obvious to Hume, that his argument for a sceptical conclusion is entirely unaffected if we substitute 'universal-' for 'predictive-' in the conclusion (j) of stage 2; if, in other words, that stage of his argument is adapted so as to concern inductive inferences with conclusions such as 'All flames are hot.' But now, as has also been remarked, (j) is itself a universal proposition. Hence if it were also factual, i.e. itself just such another proposition as 'All flames are hot', then Hume's sceptical conclusion would say, *concerning itself*, that it is 'not reason' which ever 'engages' us to believe it. And that, certainly, is the precise opposite of what Hume thought! On this ground too, therefore, a factual interpretation of Hume's sceptical conclusion is excluded.

To determine positively what kind of proposition (j) is, let us again use stage 1 of Hume's argument, and its conclusion (d), as a stalking-horse. That (d), 'All *a priori* inferences are unreasonable', is not a factual proposition, we now know. There is indeed, as was pointed out earlier in this section, a factual proposition about the *a priori* inference which Hume repeatedly affirms. This was, that knowledge of its premiss ('This is a flame') does not suffice to produce any belief in its conclusion ('This is hot'), in our minds as a matter of fact. And by contrast with this factual proposition, it is not hard to see what Hume was doing in stage 1 of his argument. He was considering the same inference, not now from the point of view of fact, but from the point of view of reason. He was asking not, how *do* we infer from 'This is a flame', but how *would* we, 'if reason determined us'?[4] In other words, Hume was asking: what degree of belief, if any, in the conclusion of an *a priori* inference, would be produced by a knowledge of its premiss, in a completely rational inferrer?

Any answer to that question would be an assessment of the degree of conclusiveness of the *a priori* inference; that is, a certain statement of logical probability. The conclusion (d) is Hume's answer to it. Consequently (d) is a statement of logical probability.

Similarly (j), we know, is not a factual proposition. There is indeed, as we have seen, a factual proposition about the predictive-inductive inference which Hume repeatedly affirms. This was, that knowledge of *its* premisses (unlike knowledge of the premiss of the *a priori* inference) *is* sufficient for a certain degree of belief in, and

---

[4] *Treatise*, p. 89.

even for 'the last degree of assurance' about, the conclusion 'This is hot'. Now by contrast with this factual proposition, it is clear that in stage 2 of his argument, Hume is considering the predictive-inductive inference, not from the point of view of fact, but from the point of view of reason. He is asking here, not how men *do* infer from 'This is a flame and all of the many flames observed in the past have been hot', but how *would* they, if reason were 'the guide of life'.[5] In other words, Hume was asking: what degree of belief, if any, in the conclusion of a predictive-inductive inference, would accompany knowledge of its premiss in a completely rational inferrer?

But any answer to that question would be an assessment of the degree of conclusiveness of the predictive-inductive inference; that is, a certain statement of logical probability. The conclusion (j) is Hume's answer to it. Consequently (j), his predictive-inductive scepticism, is a statement of logical probability.

(ii) The sceptical content of this statement of logical probability

The next question, given that this is the kind of proposition that (j) is, concerns the specific content of (j). *What* assessment of the conclusiveness of predictive-inductive inferences does Hume's sceptical conclusion make? More particularly, is it possible to capture the specifically sceptical content of (j) in one of the more definite of the various types of statements of logical probability which we distinguished in Chapter 1 above?

The more definite types of statements of logical probability, it will be recalled, are those that I called respectively numerical and comparative equalities and inequalities. It would strain credibility if I were to try to show that Hume's conclusion (j) is really a certain numerical equality. But it can indeed be shown, what is perhaps scarcely less surprising, that there is a certain *comparative* equality which embodies a large part at least of the sceptical content of Hume's conclusion.

It is to be observed, first, that although Hume's two conclusions (d) and (j), about the *a priori* and the predictive-inductive inference respectively, are both adverse, only the second is sceptical: that is, shockingly contrary to common belief, and unfavourable to men's pretensions to knowledge. Men in general, as we have seen that Hume stresses, tacitly make not only a favourable 'classificatory'

[5] *Abstract*, p. 294.

assessment of the conclusiveness of the predictive-inductive inference, but they in effect ascribe to it the highest possible degree of conclusiveness. And Hume's conclusion, whatever precise content we are to attach to the epithet 'unreasonable', is certainly some assessment of the predictive-inductive inference which is sharply contrary to that common one. But his assessment (d) of the conclusiveness of the *a priori* inference, viz. that it is unreasonable, is, on the other hand, no different from that which other men make —as Hume himself stresses, and as is in any case obvious.

Now, what is that assessment? What degree of conclusiveness do men in general agree in ascribing to the *a priori* inference? To this, Hume's answer is quite clear, at least in comparative terms. Men, he says, are no more inclined, by the first flame they observe, towards belief in 'This is hot', than they are by a total absence of experience of any kind;[6] though of course not less either. It is only experience of the constant conjunction of heat with flame that, on the observation of a further flame, produces belief in 'This is hot'. Men in general, then, according to Hume, regard the *a priori* inference as neither more nor less conclusive than an inference to the same conclusion from premisses which are entirely devoid of (what experience alone can supply) factual content. In other words, abbreviating in the usual way, Hume ascribed to men in general the following statement of logical probability:

(1) P(This is hot, This is a flame.t) = P(This is hot, t).

And about the *a priori* inference, as we have seen, Hume's conclusion (d) agrees with what other men believe; he was not intending to ascribe *more* conclusiveness (or, of course, less) to the *a priori* inference than others do! We must, therefore, ascribe to Hume, as being part at least of what he means by calling the *a priori* inference 'unreasonable', the statement of logical probability (1).[7]

Next, it is certain, quite independently of any interpretation or even translation of Hume's argument, that what he concluded in (j) about the predictive-inductive inference was at any rate the same as he had concluded earlier in (d) about the *a priori* inference. Once

---

[6] All the versions of stage 1 of Hume's argument will bear this statement out. The clearest expression by Hume, however, of his ascription to men in general of the proposition (1) about to be mentioned, will be found on pp. 29–30 of the *Enquiry*.

[7] It was, therefore, no accident of terminology, but on the contrary an expression of something Hume believed (viz. (1)), that he should have called the *a priori* inference an inference 'without', or 'before we have had' experience, notwithstanding that its premiss is an observation-statement.

Its sceptical content

(d) and (j) are identified as being statements of logical probability, therefore, there is at least one further comparative equality which we must ascribe to Hume. This is, that the degree of conclusiveness of the predictive-inductive inference is the same as that of the *a priori* inference. Or (abbreviating the primary propositions in an obvious way, and for the sake of brevity abridging the 'many' observed flames to two), we must ascribe to Hume the statement of logical probability:

(2) $P(\text{Hot } a, \text{Flame } a.\text{Hot } b.\text{Flame } b.\text{Hot } c.\text{Flame } c.t)$
$= P(\text{Hot } a, \text{Flame } a.t)$.

This proposition would perhaps serve as expressing the content of (j). But a still better suggestion emerges if we take (2) along with the earlier statement of logical probability which Hume endorsed, and which when similarly abbreviated reads:

(1) $P(\text{Hot } a, \text{Flame } a.t) = P(\text{Hot } a, t)$.

For (1) and (2) now entail:

(3) $P(\text{Hot } a, \text{Flame } a.\text{Hot } b.\text{Flame } b.\text{Hot } c.\text{Flame } c.t)$
$= P(\text{Hot } a, t)$.

And here indeed is a statement of logical probability which clearly expresses the sceptical content of Hume's conclusion (j). Or rather, since (3) may not exhaust the meaning of saying that the predictive-inductive inference is 'unreasonable', we must say that (3) is at least part of the content of Hume's sceptical conclusion, and a part of it big enough to partake of the sceptical character of the whole. Hume's predictive-inductive scepticism, then, is a judgement of 'irrelevance' in Keynes's sense: in particular, it asserts the irrelevance of experience, as we may say, to the initial probability of predictive conclusions.

(iii) Hume's first suppressed premiss as a statement of logical probability

Hume's sceptical conclusion (3) is a comparative equality. No comparative equality, we saw in Chapter 1 section (*vii*), can be proved empirically. If a comparative equality is validly inferred, therefore, it can only be from premisses some at least of which are themselves statements of logical probability. Hume's conclusion was validly inferred from his premisses. Hence some of them too, as well as his conclusion, must be statements of logical probability.

One such is the first suppressed premiss of the argument: 'No contingent propositions can be validly inferred from necessarily true premises.' Clearly, this is a judgement of invalidity. It asserts the invalidity of every argument from necessarily true premises to contingent conclusions. Consequently this premiss has, as at least part of its content, the statement of logical probability:

(4) If h is contingent, $P(h, t) < 1$.

This is a very general statement of initial logical probability, and an especially interesting one. For it will be recognized (from Chapter 1 section (vi)), as being Carnap's requirement, for adequate measures of logical probability, that they be 'regular'. I will accordingly refer to (4), which will be very important later in the evaluation of Hume's argument, as 'the Regularity premiss' of that argument.

(iv) The fallibilist consequence as a statement of logical probability

From the Regularity premiss and Hume's two stated premisses, the most that follows, we have seen, is that all predictive-inductive inferences are invalid, and that the inferences which result when their premisses are supplemented by further observational ones are likewise invalid. This, the fallibilist consequence, is clearly, as has been remarked earlier, a general judgement of invalidity; or rather, it is two such judgements. It too, therefore, is a statement of logical probability, viz.:

(5) If h and e_1 are such that the inference from e_1 to h is predictive-inductive, $P(h, e_1.t) < 1$; and if e_2 is observational, $P(h, e_1.e_2.t) < 1$.

(v) The deductivist premiss as a statement of logical probability

In order to make Hume's argument from the fallibilist consequence to his sceptical conclusion a valid one, we found it necessary to ascribe to him a further unstated premiss, that of deductivism: 'All invalid arguments are unreasonable.' But if Hume's conception of an unreasonable inference was correctly specified, at least in part, as it has been specified in (1) and (3) above, then part at least of the content of his deductivist premiss is contained in the following statement of logical probability:

(6) If e and h are such that e does not entail h, $P(h, e.t) = P(h, t)$.

(vi) Generalization of the sceptical conclusion and fallibilist consequence

It is obvious, as was remarked earlier, that stage 2 of Hume's argument is altogether unaffected if we substitute in its conclusion

Generalization

(j) 'universal-inductive' for 'predictive-inductive' inference; that is, if we make that stage of the argument concern, instead of predictive-inductive inferences, the class of inferences of which 'All of the many observed flames have been hot, so, all flames are hot' is a paradigm. It is equally obvious that Hume knew this, and that he intended the sceptical conclusion which he drew about predictive-inductive inferences to be drawn also about universal-inductive ones. If, then, the nature and at least part of the content of his predictive inductive scepticism are correctly represented by (3) above, then we must also ascribe to Hume a 'universal-inductive scepticism', i.e.:

(7) If e and h are such that the inference from e to h is universal-inductive, $P(h, e.t) = P(h, t)$.

But of course even (3) and (7) together do not exhaust the range of the scepticism about inductive inference which Hume intended his argument to lead to. It is not as though he thought that there are other inductive inferences which are more conclusive than either the predictive- or the universal-inductive inference. His scepticism extended, and of course has always been understood to extend, to 'all reasoning from experience'.[8] Hume's inductive scepticism, therefore, is general inductive scepticism; i.e. the judgement of irrelevance, much more general than (3) or (7):

(8) If e and h are such that the inference from e to h is inductive, $P(h, e.t) = P(h, t)$.

For the same reason, Hume's inductive fallibilism is not confined, any more than his inductive scepticism is, to the special case of the predictive-inductive inference. We ought therefore to ascribe to him the judgement of invalidity which generalizes (5) in just the same way as (8) generalizes (3) and (7); that is, general inductive fallibilism:

(9) If e_1 and h are such that the inference from e_1 to h is inductive, $P(h, e_1.t) < 1$; and if e_2 is observational, $P(h, e_1.e_2.t) < 1$.

(vii) The essence of Hume's argument for general inductive scepticism

When, therefore, Hume's argument for inductive scepticism is generalized in a way in which he certainly intended it to be

[8] *Abstract*, p. 294.

Its further interpretation and generalization

generalized, it can be summed up as follows. Hume drew the sceptical conclusion

(8) For all inductive arguments from e to h, $P(h, e.t) = P(h, t)$

from premisses which entail at most, about inductive arguments, the fallibilist consequence

(9) $P(h, e.t) < 1$,

taken together with the deductivist assumption

(6) For all invalid arguments from e to h, $P(h, e.t) = P(h, t)$.

Part Three
HUME'S ARGUMENT FOR INDUCTIVE
SCEPTICISM: EVALUATION

GLOSSARY OF THESES

It may be helpful to the reader to bring together here for reference, all the various theses to be discussed in Part Three.

The main ones are the following:

Hume's Inductive Scepticism (8): For all e and h such that the argument from e to h is inductive, $P(h, e.t) = P(h, t)$.

Deductivism (6): For all e and h such that the argument from e to h is invalid, $P(h, e.t) = P(h, t)$.

Inductive Fallibilism (9): For all e_1, e_2 and h such that the argument from e_1 to h is inductive and e_2 is observational, $P(h, e_1.t) < 1$ and $P(h, e_1.e_2.t) < 1$.

These three theses are the subjects respectively of Chapters 5, 6, and 7.

Two other theses referred to fairly often in what follows are:

the *Thesis of Regularity*: For all contingent h, $P(h, t) < 1$.

the *Fundamental Thesis of the Theory of Logical Probability*: There exist e_1, e_2, h_1, h_2 such that $P(h_1, e_1.t) < 1$, $P(h_2, e_2.t) < 1$, and $P(h_1, e_1.t) \neq P(h_2, e_2.t)$.

5

THE FALSITY OF ITS SCEPTICAL CONCLUSION

(i) The currency of Hume's inductive scepticism

The argument identified above was not expected by its author to have the effect of producing in his readers belief in its sceptical conclusion. The confidence which men (and some animals) repose in inductive inference, Hume thought, has its roots in a level of organic existence much too deep to be disturbed by philosophical arguments. Even more generally, Hume says, it is characteristic of 'arguments . . . merely sceptical, . . . *that they admit of no answer and produce no conviction*'.[1] Whether or not these generalizations are true, it seems to have been true, at least during the eighteenth and nineteenth centuries, that Hume's argument had no success in bringing about belief in inductive scepticism, or even in commanding attention for it.

The situation now, however, is very different. The vulgar, of course, still suppose that the inductive sciences are the offspring of observation and reasonable inference. But among the learned it is no longer the eccentricity of a solitary thinker, but rather a well-marked though minor tendency of thought, to suppose that on the contrary those sciences owe their existence to men's attachment to a kind of inference which sets logic or reason at defiance. This supposition is not made widely, deeply, or steadily, even among philosophers. But that it is often made, must be obvious to every reader of recent philosophy. This fact is just one expression of the enormous influence which, in the last fifty years, Hume's philosophy of science has acquired.

Of all contemporary philosophers of science, it is Karl Popper who gives his readers the general impression of coming closest to a full and clear acceptance of Hume's inductive scepticism. That this

[1] *Enquiry*, p. 155. Hume's italics.

general impression is correct, is confirmed, in the light of Chapters 2–4 above, by an interesting passage in one of the new appendices added to the English translation of his classic book.[2] Here Popper discusses a certain statement of logical probability which is an obvious special case of what I have identified as being Hume's inductive scepticism (8): viz. '$P(Fa, Fb.t) = P(Fa, t)$' (in which F is an observational predicate). And this proposition Popper regards as being both true and the upshot of 'Hume's criticism of induction'.[3]

(ii) The nature of possible arguments against it

What would constitute an 'answer to Hume' concerning induction? More specifically, what would constitute a proof of the falsity of his inductive scepticism? It is not possible to answer these questions before one has a clear and correct answer to the prior question, 'What *is* Hume's inductive scepticism?' My answer to this is at least clear: viz. (8) '$P(h, e.t) = P(h, t)$ for all inductive arguments from e to h'. And if it is also correct, then an answer to the above question is not far to seek. A proof is at least a valid argument from true premisses. What is needed, then, is at least a valid argument from true premisses to some conclusion inconsistent with (8).

But, as we saw in Chapter 1 section (*vii*), the falsity of a statement of logical probability can be proved empirically—validly derived, that is, from observational premisses—only under very special conditions. One of these was, that the statement of logical probability in question must be a judgement of validity. But inductive scepticism (8) is not a judgement of validity. Consequently its falsity can be proved, if at all, only in the way in which the falsity of a false statement of logical probability can in general be proved. That is, by a valid derivation of a statement of logical probability inconsistent with it, from true premisses which must include other statements of logical probability.

Clearly, however, not every such derivation proves the falsity of a statement inconsistent with its conclusion. For that, the premisses must in addition be *obviously* true. Now, in considering possible proofs of the falsity of (8), this requirement presents no difficulty with respect to those premisses which are principles of logical

---

[2] *The Logic of Scientific Discovery* (London, 1959), starred appendix vii, pp. 367–70.
[3] Ibid. p. 369. My italics. (Popper here writes statements of initial logical probability 'unconditionally', and also uses unanalysed, or at most subscripted, abbreviations for the primary propositions. Thus he writes the above judgement of irrelevance, for example (p. 368), '$P(a) = P(a, b)$'.)

probability. Any principle of logical probability is certainly sufficiently obvious to function as a premiss in a proof of falsity of a statement of logical probability. But what of those premisses which are themselves statements of logical probability? How obvious must the truth of one statement of logical probability be, before it can properly be used as a premiss in proving the falsity of other such statements?

I will not attempt a general answer to this question, but content myself instead with advancing a certain condition as being at any rate sufficient. A statement of logical probability will have been proved false, I suggest, if its falsity has been shown to follow from premisses which contain (apart from principles) only the weakest of all numerical inequalities, viz. judgements of invalidity, all of which concern arguments of extreme simplicity and obvious invalidity. More specifically still, a statement of logical probability will have been proved false, I suggest, if its falsity has been shown to follow from two judgements of regularity, $P(h_1, t) < 1$ and $P(h_2, t) < 1$, where h_1 and h_2 are contingent propositions free from quantifiers.

I believe that this will be accepted as a sufficient condition for premisses to be obvious enough to be used to prove the falsity of a statement of logical probability. It will be hard indeed, otherwise, to see how any false statement of logical probability could ever be proved false. Yet, as was observed in Chapter 1 section (*vii*), they certainly can be.

The argument to be given in the next section, against Hume's inductive scepticism (8), is one which satisfies the above condition. As far as I know, this argument is new. But there is another argument, which I think is also a valid one from true premisses to a conclusion inconsistent with (8), which has been known, in a sense, for a very long time. That argument is Laplace's 'inversion of Bernoulli's Theorem'. I say it has been known for a long time 'in a sense', because although there is a vague tradition to the effect that Laplace's argument refutes inductive scepticism, the argument has never to my knowledge been presented in such a way as to make clear the nature and content of either its premisses or its conclusion. The main obstacle to such a presentation, beyond doubt, is the unparalleled amount of confusion which surrounds the nature and content of the 'Theorems' of Bernoulli themselves. These propositions have been conceived in the most various ways possible: as mathematical truths; as empirical laws; as principles of logical probability; and again as statements of logical probability. (Textual support for each of the last three interpretations, for example, can be found in no less a place than Part V of Keynes's *Treatise*.) If, though only if, the last-mentioned of these interpretations of Bernoulli's Theorems is correct,[4] then the nature and validity of Laplace's famous 'inversion' argument become clear. And if the 'Theorem' in question is true, then its inversion is a valid argument from one true statement of logical probability to another which is inconsistent with inductive scepticism (8). Even on those two suppositions, however, Laplace's argument would not be a proof of the falsity of (8), at least under the condition advanced above as being sufficient for such a proof. For its premiss would be an extremely *strong* statement of logical probability, about a rather *complex* argument; unlike the premisses of the argument about to be given.

(iii) Von Thun's argument against Hume's inductive scepticism

(The propositions which are principles of logical probability are numbered (P1) etc.; those which are statements, (S1) etc.)

We assume the following principles.

(P1) The conjunction principle, $P(q.r, p) = P(q, p) \times P(r, p.q)$.

(P2) The negation principle, $P(q, p) = 1 - P(\sim q, p)$.

(P3) The equivalence principle (that logically equivalent propositions can be substituted for one another *salva probabilitate* in statements and in principles of logical probability).

(P4) The lower-limit principle, $P(q, p) \geq 0$.

Now, let the predicate F be observational. Then the argument from Fa to $Fb.Fa$ is inductive. From (P1) it follows that

(P5) $P(Fa.(Fb.Fa), t) = P(Fa, t) \times P(Fb.Fa, Fa.t)$.

Whence, with (P3), it follows that

(P6) $P(Fb.Fa, t) = P(Fa, t) \times P(Fb.Fa, Fa.t)$.

From (P2) and (P3),

(P7) If $P(Fb.Fa, t) = 0$ then $P(\sim Fb \vee \sim Fa, t) = 1$.

---

[4] As Carnap (*Foundations*, pp. 498 ff.) simply assumes; although really a great deal of argument is needed in order to exclude the other interpretations, and especially the view of Bernoulli's Theorems as *principles* of logical probability. The beginning of such argument is given in my 'Misconditionalisation', *The Australasian Journal of Philosophy*, vol. 50, no. 2, 1972.

From (P2), (P4) and (P6),

(P8) If $P(Fb.Fa, t) \neq 0$, then (each term in (P6) is > 0 and ≤ 1, and) either $P(Fa, t) = 1$ or $P(Fb.Fa, Fa.t) > P(Fb.Fa, t)$.

Consequently, from (P7) and (P8),

(P9) Either $P(\sim Fb \vee \sim Fa, t) = 1$ or $P(Fa, t) = 1$ or $P(Fb.Fa, Fa.t) > P(Fb.Fa, t)$.

But

(S1) $P(\sim Fb \vee \sim Fa, t) < 1$

and

(S2) $P(Fa, t) < 1$.

Consequently

(S3) $P(Fb.Fa, Fa.t) > P(Fb.Fa, t)$.

But, since Hume's inductive scepticism (8) entails that $P(Fb.Fa, Fa.t) = P(Fb.Fa, t)$, (S3) is inconsistent with Hume's inductive scepticism.

Apart from the principles (P1)–(P4), the only premisses used in this argument are the statements of logical probability (S1) and (S2).[5] Each of these is a weak statement, a numerical inequality, and at that a numerical inequality of the weakest kind: a judgement of invalidity. In fact, (S1) and (S2) are mere judgements of regularity, each of which says, concerning an argument from tautological premises to a (non-quantified) contingent conclusion, just that its degree of conclusiveness is at any rate less than the highest possible degree. Consequently von Thun's argument is a proof of the falsity of Hume's inductive scepticism.

This argument is not only sufficient but may actually be more than is necessary to refute Hume's inductive scepticism: for it should be noticed that it would still refute Hume's inductive scepticism even if that thesis were not (8), but any one of a certain number of propositions considerably weaker than (8). Suppose that my interpretation of Hume's argument in Chapter 4 above was mistaken,

[5] This is not *strictly* true. For in the step from (P5) to (P6) I have assumed the logical equivalence of $Fa.(Fb.Fa)$ and $Fb.Fa$; and similarly in (P7) I have assumed the logical equivalence of $\sim(Fb.Fa)$ and $\sim Fb \vee \sim Fa$. Now, judgements of logical equivalence are conjunctions of judgements of validity, and are therefore themselves (conjunctions of) statements of logical probability. All of the four judgements of validity involved here, however, are so extremely obviously true, that to have made them explicit would have been to encumber the presentation of the argument to no purpose.

and that Hume was not in fact discussing the logical probability of inductive arguments. Suppose that the property of inductive arguments which Hume was assessing, was not their logical probability, but their 'rationality'; that is, some non-empirical magnitude, belonging to arguments, but distinct from degree of conclusiveness. (That there are such magnitudes, is certain: for example, what Keynes called the 'weight' of arguments.)[6] On this supposition, Hume's sceptical conclusion about all arguments from e to h which are inductive would be, not the statement of logical probability (8), but the 'statement of rationality': $R(h, e.t) = R(h, t)$. Now, of course, von Thun's argument does not refute this 'proposition', because so far almost nothing has been said to make the concept of rationality determinate; we do not yet know what properties we are to credit this magnitude with. What von Thun's argument shows is that if rationality has all the properties of—that is, is identical with—logical probability, then Hume's inductive scepticism is false. What may not be obvious is that his argument would suffice to refute Hume's inductive scepticism, as long as 'rationality' were *like* logical probability in the following two respects: that it is a strictly monotonic function of logical probability (i.e. that $P(q, p) > P(s, r)$ if and only if $R(q, p) > R(s, r)$); and that the rationality of an argument does not attain its upper limit if the argument has tautological premises and a non-quantified contingent conclusion. For under these conditions our present premises (P1)–(P4) will entail a disjunctive analogue of (P9) for rationality; and its first two disjuncts will still be able to be negated by true judgements of 'non-maximal rationality'. Then it will follow, corresponding to the present (S3), that $R(Fb.Fa, Fa.t) > R(Fb.Fa, t)$; and thus even the more cautious or indeterminate version of Hume's inductive scepticism which was suggested above will have been refuted. This consideration is important, because it shows that von Thun's argument still finds its mark even when considerable allowance has been made for error on my part in deciding what Hume's inductive scepticism *is*.

Another feature of von Thun's argument which is worthy of notice is this: that by it we arrive at a very interesting result from principles of logical probability alone, before any statements of logical probability have been asserted.[7] This is the principle (P9).

---

[6] Cf. *Treatise*, Ch. VI.

[7] Apart, that is, from the extremely obvious judgements of validity referred to in note 5 above.

For what (P9) shows is that Hume's inductive scepticism requires a violation of regularity. In other words (to use the terminology of Chapter 1 section (*viii*) above), (P9) shows that if one departs from the natural assessment of the conclusiveness of inductive inferences in the direction of scepticism, one must make another, unanticipated, departure from natural assessments, only this time in the direction of credulity, concerning certain other (non-inductive) inferences. And not just an assessment of those inferences which is slightly more favourable than most men would make; for the cost of Hume's inductive scepticism, (P9) shows, is that one must ascribe, either to an argument from a tautology to 'This is a flame', say, or to an argument from a tautology to 'This or that is not a flame', *the highest possible degree of conclusiveness*!

More generally, (P9) is interesting for the light it throws on a suggestion which is sometimes made, though on what grounds is not usually clear, that 'inductive logic' in the Carnapian sense requires the admission of 'the synthetic *a priori*': that is, requires the thesis that at least some factual propositions can be known *a priori*. Now, to assert that propositions such as 'This is a flame' or 'This or that is not a flame' can be inferred from a tautology with the highest possible degree of conclusiveness, would certainly be to say that they can be known *a priori*. Consequently (P9) has the merit of showing that it is Hume's inductive scepticism, *not its denial*, which requires the admission of the synthetic *a priori*.

(*iv*) *The* ad hominem *position in the light of this argument*

Von Thun's argument is a proof that inductive scepticism (8) is false. That it is such a proof is entirely independent, of course, of the question who, if any one, has held (8), or on what grounds. But (8) was in fact held by Hume, and it is especially interesting, in the light of the von Thun argument, to recall the grounds on which Hume held it.

For on the one hand, the only premisses of von Thun's argument (apart from some principles of logical probability and some extremely obvious judgements of validity) were the two judgements of regularity, (S1) and (S2). And on the other hand, it will be recalled, one of the (suppressed) premisses of Hume's argument for inductive scepticism was the regularity premiss (4), '$P(h, t) < 1$ for all contingent h'. But this means that von Thun's argument *against* Hume's inductive scepticism (8) has for its main premisses two propositions which are deducible from a proposition which Hume not only accepted, but actually employed as a premiss in his argument *for* (8). Both Hume's argument for (8), and von Thun's argument against it, are valid. Consequently von Thun's argument, as well as showing the falsity of Hume's conclusion, also shows that Hume's premisses, conjoined with some of the principles of logical probability, are *inconsistent*.

Apart from the deductivist premiss (6), it will be recalled, Hume's only premisses were (e), (f), and the regularity premiss (4), which together entail, and entail no more than, inductive fallibilism (9). Thus the strongest conjunction of statements of logical probability to which Hume's premisses commit him is the conjunction of (4), (6), and (9). ((4) $P(h, t) < 1$ for all contingent h; (6) $P(h, e.t) = P(h, t)$ if the argument from e to h is invalid; (9) $P(h, e_1.t) < 1$ and $P(h, e_1.e_2.t) < 1$ if the argument from e_1 to h is inductive and e_2 is observational.) Thus, this conjunction of statements of logical probability is shown by the von Thun argument to be inconsistent with the principles of logical probability.

This criticism of Hume's argument for inductive scepticism (8) is, of course, no more than an *ad hominem* one; i.e., an argument for (8), which was different from Hume's argument, would not necessarily be exposed to it. Just how serious a criticism it nevertheless is, may not be immediately obvious. For it might be thought, in particular, that it would be open to Hume to avoid inconsistency, while still maintaining (4), (6), and (9), simply by rejecting one or more of the principles of logical probability (P1)–(P4), which were used as premisses in von Thun's argument. But that is not so.

If there is someone who makes no statements of logical probability whatever, it may be possible for him to reject some or all of the principles of logical probability. It is no part of the object of this book, as was said at the beginning, to try to establish any of them; but in any case we are not here dealing with such a person. We are dealing with Hume, and he, as has been shown, is committed to a number of statements of logical probability. And no one who is thus committed is at liberty to reject the principles of logical probability.

The reason is, that without the principles of logical probability (as was said in Chapter 1 section (i)), statements of logical probability are 'blind'. That is, it is the principles, and they alone, which inform us what the consequences are of any given statement of logical

The ad hominem *position in the light of this argument* 73

probability. Consequently any one who denied the principles, while making a statement of logical probability, would be committing himself, despite the appearances, to nothing determinate whatever. In such circumstances, in other words, the possibility would vanish of any criticism whatever of any given statements of logical probability.

In particular, without the principles, one could never be in a position to say that a given statement of logical probability had, as one of its consequences, the falsity of another; i.e., that two statements of logical probability are inconsistent. For there is, strictly, no inconsistency between, for example, $P(A, B) = \frac{1}{2}$ and $P(\sim A, B) = 1$. There is only the inconsistency of their conjunction with the negation principle. There is, strictly, no inconsistency between $P(A, B) = \frac{1}{2}$ and $P(A, B) < \frac{1}{2}$; or again between (S3) $P(Fb.Fa, Fa.t) > P(Fb.Fa, t)$, and the Humean $P(Fb.Fa, Fa.t) = P(Fb.Fa, t)$. There is only the inconsistency of their conjunction with a certain principle of logical probability (viz. the uniqueness principle, that no argument has more than one degree of logical probability). In fact, inconsistency with one or more of the principles of logical probability is all that ever is or can be meant by speaking of two statements of logical probability as being inconsistent with one another.

Hume, then, having asserted some statements of logical probability, is not at liberty to reject the principles of logical probability.[8] Consequently the full *ad hominem* effect of the von Thun argument is this: that, in the only sense in which statements of logical probability can be inconsistent, it shows that Hume's deductivism (6), regularity (4), and inductive fallibilism (9) (taken with the extremely obvious judgements of validity mentioned in note 5 above) are inconsistent statements of logical probability. For they entail both Hume's inductive scepticism (8), and a statement (S3) inconsistent with (8). Contrary, then, to the assumption which in Chapter 4 section (*i*) above was tentatively made in Hume's favour, the premisses of his argument for inductive scepticism are actually inconsistent.

---

[8] The last two paragraphs apply equally, of course, to factual probability. One who appears to assert some statements, while denying the principles, of factual probability, actually evacuates the content of the former.

6

THE FALSITY OF ITS DEDUCTIVIST PREMISS

(i) The relation of deductivism to certain other theses
If Hume's argument for inductive scepticism is, as I have tried to show it is, valid but with a false conclusion, it must have a false premiss. Deductivism (6) is one of the premisses, and in this chapter I try to show (section *(iv)*) that it is false. A necessary preliminary, however, both to the arguments against deductivism, and to the discussion in section *(ii)* of the currency of that thesis among philosophers, is a clear view of the logical relation of deductivism to certain other theses. And first, what is the relation between deductivism and inductive scepticism; between, that is, the statements of logical probability (6), 'P($h, e.t$) = P(h, t) if the argument from e to h is invalid', and (8), 'P($h, e.t$) = P(h, t) if the argument from e to h is inductive'?

It will be evident that both of these propositions could be true. It should be equally evident that both could be false. But it is also possible for deductivism to be true and inductive scepticism false. For there is nothing in the content of (6) itself to tell us that the class of invalid arguments includes all arguments from observed to unobserved instances of empirical predicates. Inductive scepticism (8) follows from (6) conjoined with the thesis of inductive fallibilism (9), not from (6) alone. Finally, the falsity of deductivism is consistent with the truth of inductive scepticism. For there could be some invalid arguments from e to h such that P($h, e.t$) $\neq$ P(h, t), without there being, among these arguments, any inductive ones. The logical relation, consequently, between deductivism and inductive scepticism, is independence.

This result, even though half of it—the non-deducibility of (8) from (6)—was made clear in Chapter 3, is somewhat surprising. One expects the relation between deductivism and inductive

The relation of deductivism to other theses

scepticism to be closer, and more positive, than independence. For this mistaken expectation, the influence of the Carnapian usage of 'inductive' may be partly responsible. For 'inductive' in that usage is synonymous with 'invalid', and then, of course, (6) and (8), far from being independent, are obviously equivalent.

There are, however, much deeper causes than this for the tendency to think that the two theses are more closely related than they are in reality. One is the fact that deductivism is widely and correctly, even if indistinctly, believed to be a premiss in the only argument which is known for inductive scepticism (viz. Hume's). A second is the fact that the thesis which, when conjoined with (6), does allow the derivation of (8), viz. inductive fallibilism (9), is one which has become second nature to us. (That it has become so, must be ascribed to the influence of Hume. Cf. Chapters 7–8 below.) A third fact which helps to obscure the independence of deductivism and inductive scepticism, is the following: that inductive inferences are the only ones of which philosophers nowadays are vividly aware, both that they are all invalid, and that the natural assessments of them are in many cases extremely favourable. This state of affairs must, again, be ascribed partly to the influence of Hume; but not wholly. It must partly be ascribed to the circumstance that very few philosophers or logicians have ever taken much interest in statistical inference, or in the kinds of inference which men constantly make in connection with games of chance. All of the inferences which I called 'Bernoullian', for example (Chapter 1, section (*ix*)), are invalid, although the natural assessment of many of them is extremely favourable; yet compared with the philosophical literature concerning inductive inference, the philosophical literature concerning Bernoullian inference is almost non-existent. And the effect of this circumstance is that the only class of inferences, which is immediately recognized by most philosophers as being doomed by deductivism to sceptical assessment, is that which consists of inductive inferences. This, I suggest, is the main reason why we are apt mistakenly to suppose that there is a close connection between deductivism and inductive scepticism.

In fact, however, they are logically independent. In particular, inductive scepticism is not 'a special case of' deductivism: it is *not* part of the content of the deductivist thesis. This fact will be important in section (*iv*) below; as will the fact that the *potential* sceptical consequences of deductivism (once it is conjoined with appropriate judgements of invalidity), are by no means confined to induction.

I turn now to the relation between deductivism (6), and what I earlier called (Chapter 1 section (*ii*) 'the fundamental thesis of the theory of logical probability': the thesis, that is, that one argument may be more conclusive than another even though both are invalid.

This thesis and deductivism (6) cannot both be false. For suppose (6) false. Then there exists an argument from e to h such that $P(h, e.t) < 1$ yet $P(h, e.t) \neq P(h, t)$. But if $P(h, e.t) < 1$ then (by obvious principles of logical probability)[1] $P(h, t) < 1$. Whence two arguments exist, viz. from e to h and from t to h, both invalid but of unequal logical probability. Thus, if deductivism is false then the fundamental thesis of the theory of logical probability is true.

The two theses are not, however, inconsistent. Their consistency would be proved if it were proved that two arguments, from e_1 to h_1 and from e_2 to h_2, can satisfy the following conditions: that $P(h_1, e_1.t) < 1$ and $P(h_2, e_2.t) < 1$; that $P(h_1, e_1.t) = P(h_1, t)$ and $P(h_2, e_2.t) = P(h_2, t)$; and that $P(h_1, e_1.t) \neq P(h_2, e_2.t)$. For the first and third conditions would ensure the truth of the fundamental thesis of the theory of logical probability; while the first and second would ensure that deductivism has not been negated. Two arguments can satisfy these conditions. For let h_1 be $Fa.Ga$; h_2 be Fa; and let e_1 and e_2 both be Hb. Then all the three conditions are satisfied. Thus deductivism and the fundamental thesis of the theory of logical probability can both be true, although they cannot both be false. In short they are sub-contraries.

This result is, like the earlier one in this section, somewhat surprising. One would rather expect deductivism to be, if not the contradictory, at least a contrary of the fundamental thesis of the theory of logical probability. And, again as in the earlier case, there is a deep reason for the mistake, one which even goes far to excuse it. This is the fact that the deductivism which is a suppressed premiss of Hume's argument admits of another interpretation than (6), and one according to which it is indeed inconsistent with the fundamental thesis of the theory of logical probability. For it would be very natural to interpret 'All invalid arguments are unreasonable' as meaning that all invalid arguments have *the same* degree of conclusiveness. And in that case, of course, the logical relation in question is in fact contradiction. This interpretation is in fact not

[1] e.g. by theorem 9, Keynes's *Treatise*, p. 140.

The relation of deductivism to other theses

only natural but almost inevitable before the identification of Hume's argument is carried as far as it has been carried in Chapter 4 above.[2] Once it has been carried so far, however, the attribution to Hume of any version of deductivism stronger than (6) is not necessary to make his argument valid, and therefore would be unjustified.

In fact, however, the logical relation between the fundamental thesis of the theory of logical probability, and Hume's suppressed deductivist premiss, is sub-contrariety. This fact will be made use of in sections (*ii*) and (*iv*) below.

(*ii*) *The currency of deductivism*

The object of this section is to show that the currency of deductivism is deep, wide, and long.

It must be admitted at the outset, however, that the thesis (6) has no *explicit* currency whatever. No philosopher has actually asserted that, if the argument from e to h is invalid, $P(h, e.t) = P(h, t)$. Even its less specific version, 'All invalid arguments are unreasonable', has no currency on the surface of philosophy.

Still, we were able to show, in Chapters 2–4, that deductivism, both in the less specific version and in the form of (6), really was subscribed to by Hume, for one. And, especially now, when Hume's influence and reputation are so great, it ought to be possible for a philosopher to show, without saying, that his assessment of the conclusiveness of invalid arguments is no different from Hume's. There are, in fact, several ways in which he can do so.

One way in which a contemporary philosopher can show his deductivism is the way Hume showed his. That is, by proceeding as though, when he has proved an argument invalid, he has done all that is necessary to exclude any favourable assessment of its degree of conclusiveness. This is not, as described, an infallible indication of deductivism. Conjoined with other indications, however, or given sufficient explicitness (as there was in Hume), this indication can be decisive in individual cases.

Another way is, by a philosopher's subscribing to inductive scepticism. This indicates deductivism, not because of any logical connection between the two theses; for there is none, as we saw in the preceding section. What makes it such an indication, and even

[2] For this reason I did in fact mistakenly attribute the stronger version of deductivism to Hume in my article, 'Deductivism', *Australasian Journal of Philosophy*, vol. 48, no. 1, 1970.

one which is in practice infallible to date, is the fact (also mentioned in the preceding section) that the only known argument for inductive scepticism is Hume's; an argument which does have deductivism as a premiss.

A third way in which a contemporary philosopher can show his commitment to deductivism is by rejecting the fundamental thesis of the theory of logical probability. That a philosopher does reject this thesis may, indeed, be not easy to establish with finality. But if he does, then (to avoid imputing inconsistency to him) we must impute deductivism to him. For these two theses, we have seen, cannot both be false.

Each of these indications of deductivism, I think it will be admitted, is given by some contemporary philosophers. A wholesale rejection of the theory of logical probability, for example, is certainly not an unknown attitude, or even an uncommon one, among the philosophical profession. Nor is inductive scepticism without its adherents, if what was said in Chapter 5 section (*i*) is true. And if this last indication is in practice infallible, as I have said, then deductivism has some currency, at any rate, among contemporary philosophers: viz. at least as much currency as inductive scepticism has. But since it has no surface currency, deductivism has some deep currency at present, as it had with Hume.

But I believe that this greatly understates the position, and that deductivism is in fact a thesis to which not just some but most contemporary philosophers are committed. In saying this, I go not by the first indication, since that is not decisive; nor by the second, since although inductive scepticism is a decisive indicator, the inductive sceptics are certainly not in a majority; but by the third indication, i.e. rejection of the theory of logical probability.

A deep division exists among contemporary philosophers, between those who are cultivators of the theory of logical probability or (in the Carnapian sense) 'inductive logic', and those who are not. Among the latter the very name 'inductive logic' excites contempt or indignation, and the thing itself is regarded, I think it is no exaggeration to say, as an attempt to place a fig-leaf of respectability over the naked illogicality of mankind. The attempt is considered as in itself unworthy of a philosopher, and as one the futility of which has in any case long since been exposed.[3] As one of these

---

[3] It is even widely believed, appropriately enough, that it was Hume who exposed for all time the futility of this attempt. Cf. Appendix section (*iii*).

philosophers vividly expressed it, inductive logic is simply 'the hot air of certain Renaissance publicists'.

This division among philosophers clearly must be regarded as a division between those who accept, and those who reject, the fundamental thesis of the theory of logical probability. There can be no doubt, however, which of the two groups is the more numerous. But to reject the fundamental thesis of the theory of logical probability is to be committed to deductivism. Consequently most contemporary philosophers are committed to that thesis, and the currency of deductivism, though inexplicit, is very wide.

It is also long, since it extends at least from Hume's time to ours. For it will hardly be suggested that during that time deductivism has enjoyed only an intermittent currency among philosophers. In fact, before the emergence of the theory of logical probability in the present century, there is nothing[4] which one could point to as being even an implicit and indirect rejection of deductivism.

If most contemporary philosophers are deductivists, then since they are all or almost all inductive fallibilists (cf. Chapter 7 section (*ii*)), the majority ought also to be inductive sceptics. This of course is not what one finds in fact. But if what I have said or will say concerning the currency of the three theses is true, this fact can only be interpreted as showing that most philosophers have not yet brought their philosophy of induction into a consistent state.

(*iii*) On arguments for deductivism

Before advancing arguments against deductivism, we ought to consider what has been or could be said in its favour. First, then, what arguments have actually been advanced for deductivism?

None whatever, as far as I can discover. This is in fact an inevitable consequence of the kind of currency which deductivism has long enjoyed and still widely enjoys. Hume, we know, was so far from arguing for this thesis, that he never even stated it; and the currency of deductivism, we have seen, is no more explicit in contemporary philosophers who nevertheless give every indication of embracing it. Its invariable role is that of a suppressed premiss, and if there are any other beliefs on which it is in fact grounded, they are still further than it is from ever being explicitly stated.

---

[4] Nothing, that is, within the arena of philosophy proper. But the classical theory of probability, or at least the school of Laplace, was very consciously such a rejection. Cf. Chapter 8 section (*i*) below.

Sometimes, of course, it is possible, and even easy, to say what the other beliefs are, which have disposed a philosopher to accept a certain thesis, even though the thesis has never been expressly defended by any arguments. But even this is not possible in the present case. At least, I am quite unable to suggest what if any premisses, still more deeply suppressed than deductivism, have disposed philosophers to accept that thesis.

There is only one possible exception, and this is an argument so absurd that it is only with diffidence that I will now suggest that Hume and others have been at all influenced by it. The argument in essence is this. 'Deductivism is true, *because* it conflicts with the favourable assessments which men naturally make of many invalid inferences (e.g. inductive ones).' Or still more bluntly: 'Deductivism is true, because such inaccurate assessors of the conclusiveness of inferences as men are naturally think it false.'

The argument is not entirely without foundation, because of course many natural beliefs, whether about the conclusiveness of arguments, or about matters of fact, are false. But the argument still seems, and of course really is, absurd. It cannot *follow* from the fact that a certain statement of logical probability is the natural assessment of the class of inferences in question, that it is false. For it is the natural assessment of Barbara, or *modus ponens*, for example, that they are of the highest possible degree of conclusiveness; and of course they really are so. The above argument for deductivism is therefore at any rate not valid. And since deductivism itself makes an unfavourable assessment of the conclusiveness of every other argument than a valid one, further criticism of the argument is not necessary. It is worthwhile, however, to point out its invalidity in another way. This is, that the deductivist assessment of an invalid inference is by no means the only alternative, even if we suppose that the natural assessment of it is favourable and false. Thus, if the invalid argument from e to h is inductive, for example, and the natural assessment of it is '$P(h, e.t) > P(h, t)$', this assessment may be false without the deductivist assessment being true. For the 'counter-inductive' assessment, $P(h, e.t) < P(h, t)$, may be true if the natural assessment is false, and in that case the deductivist equality is false also.

There are at least hints of the above argument in Hume: as when for example he writes that 'When I give the preference to one set of arguments above another, I do nothing but decide from my feeling

On arguments for deductivism

concerning the superiority of their influence.'[5] This at least suggests that, if I believe a certain comparative inequality, then what I believe is sufficiently discredited by the mere fact of my believing it. And contemporary philosophers must at least be suspected of having been influenced by essentially the same argument. For it is certainly often said to be 'just a fact about us', that we make the favourable assessments that we do of some invalid inferences, (certain inductive ones, for example). Now, when this is said, the use of the word 'just' in this context must mean that the inferences in question do not, in reality, have the degree of conclusiveness which men naturally take them to have. Yet does not this little word, with that momentous meaning, creep into philosophy sometimes, in contexts where all that has been previously established is that it is a fact about us, that we assess some invalid arguments favourably? I think that it does. If so, then the argument mentioned above has not been entirely without effect in disposing the minds of philosophers towards deductivism.

With this possible exception there appear to be no arguments whatever in favour of the deductivist thesis.[6]

Even if actual arguments for deductivism are wanting, it will be of interest in itself, and of importance when we come to advance some arguments against deductivism, to consider now what arguments for deductivism there *could* be (in the future, say). Given the kind of proposition that deductivism is, and also the specific content which distinguishes it from other propositions of that kind, how is the range of possible arguments in favour of it restricted?

First, from the content of deductivism it will be evident that any argument for it must be a valid one. Second, there can be no

---

[5] *Treatise*, p. 103.

[6] If this is so, it poses an interesting historical question, how to account for the wide and long currency of deductivism among philosophers. Part at least of the answer to this question must presumably lie in the great age and prestige of deductive logic. This can scarcely be the whole answer, however, if only because Hume, and indeed the whole tradition of British empiricism, from Bacon to Mill, is openly contemptuous of deductive logic. Perhaps the key to this historical question is to be found in the influence of Euclid, rather than in that of Aristotle. The idea that the degree of conclusiveness of the arguments in Euclid's geometry is the standard at which an argument ought to aim in every branch of knowledge, including empirical science, has certainly exercised an immense influence. Against it, the thesis of inductive fallibilism (9), for example, which now seems so excessively obvious, has had in fact to wage a long struggle to acquire currency. (Cf. Chapters 7-8 below.) Perhaps the currency of deductivism among philosophers is one facet of the influence of that idea.

arguments for deductivism from deductive logic. Even allowing, as one must, for some indeterminacy as to the boundaries of deductive logic, this remains true. For arguments for deductivism must be valid ones, and if there were valid arguments for it from propositions belonging to deductive logic, then there would be some branch of deductive logic of which deductivism is simply a theorem. But of course there is no such branch of deductive logic.

This ought to be obvious, yet in fact the point needs emphasis. For it seems to be often supposed that deductivism somehow has the authority of deductive logic in its favour. It is very likely of course (as was said in note 6 above) that between deductive logic, and the currency of deductivism, there is a causal, historical, connection. But that there should be any (valid) arguments from the former to the latter, is precluded by the kind of proposition that deductivism (6) is. It is a certain statement of logical probability, and neither a judgement of validity nor a judgement of invalidity. Consequently, any one who wishes to defend it, as much as one who wishes to attack it, must first of all leave the ground of deductive logic.

Third: there can be no arguments for deductivism from experience. For the only statements of logical probability (we saw in Chapter 1 section (*vii*)), of which the truth can be validly inferred from observational premisses, are judgements of invalidity. But deductivism is not a judgement of invalidity. It does not itself assert, concerning any given argument, that that argument falls within the class of arguments about which it generalizes.

What deductivism does assert, concerning every member of the class of invalid arguments, is a certain comparative equality. But we saw in Chapter 1 section (*vii*) that statements of logical probability of this kind cannot be proved true by valid inference from any premisses other than ones which include other statements of logical probability. If such a statement is to be proved, therefore, it can only be from premisses one at least of which is of a kind that can be directly discovered to be true only intuitively. A fourth restriction, consequently, on arguments for deductivism, is this: that their premisses must contain at least one statement of a kind that can be directly discovered to be true only intuitively.

These restrictions are severe. They are not more so, however, than the restrictions which we will find applying to possible arguments *against* deductivism. Nor are they (as the arguments on the other side will show), so severe as to prevent there being still a great fund of arguments which could be urged in favour of deductivism.

It must none the less be admitted that the task of finding arguments for deductivism is a daunting one, because of the extremely great strength of that thesis. Not, of course, that it belongs to the strongest kind of statement of logical probability; deductivism (6) is not a numerical equality. But it is both immensely general in its subject and extremely specific in its predicate. The class of invalid inferences is immensely wide and heterogeneous; and to say, of every such argument from e to h, that its logical probability is exactly the same as the initial logical probability of h, is to say a very great deal. It is hard indeed to think of any propositions which, while being equal to the task of entailing this one, could possibly recommend themselves to philosophers.

It will hardly need to be added, finally, that arguments for deductivism are nevertheless needed. There are, of course, very many statements of logical probability of which the truth is known without inference, directly. But it will scarcely be seriously maintained that (6), '$P(h, e.t) = P(h, t)$ if the argument from e to h is invalid', is one of those.

(iv) *Some arguments against deductivism*

The nature of the deductivist thesis, and its specific content, we have seen, impose restrictions on the range of possible arguments for it. They similarly impose restrictions on the range of possible arguments against it.

First, arguments against deductivism will have to be valid ones. This restriction flows from the specific content of deductivism, as did the same restriction on arguments for it, though not in the same way. Clearly, arguments against deductivism will need to be of a high degree of conclusiveness; but to claim this for some invalid arguments against deductivism would evidently be to beg the question against the deductivist.

Second, there can be no arguments against deductivism 'from the theory of logical probability', if that phrase is used, as it sometimes is, to refer just to the principles of logical probability. For deductivism (6) is a certain statement of logical probability, and therefore nothing inconsistent with it can be validly inferred from the principles, unaided by statements, of logical probability.

The falsity of its deductivist premiss

Third, there can be no arguments against deductivism from experience. For (as we saw in Chapter 1 section (*vii*)) the only statements of logical probability, of which the falsity can be validly inferred from observational premisses, are certain judgements of validity. But deductivism is not a judgement of validity.

Any argument against deductivism will evidently be an argument *for* a certain comparative inequality. But we saw in Chapter 1 section (*vii*) that statements of logical probability of this kind cannot be proved true by valid inference from any premisses other than ones which include other statements of logical probability. If such a statement is to be proved, therefore, it can only be from premisses one at least of which is of a kind that can be directly discovered to be true only intuitively. A fourth restriction, consequently, on arguments against deductivism is this: that their premisses must contain at least one statement of a kind that can be directly discovered to be true only intuitively.

From the preceding section it will be recalled that this restriction is one which applies also to possible arguments *for* deductivism (6). This symmetry is inevitable, since arguments against (6) will conclude with a comparative inequality, arguments for it with a comparative equality, and these two kinds of statements of logical probability are alike in that knowledge of them rests ultimately on intuition. But the symmetry also has a very important consequence. For it means that the issue between deductivism and its denial must be decided by arguments, the premisses of which cannot be discovered to be true without reliance sooner or later on *intuitive* assessments of the conclusiveness of inferences.

It is no objection, therefore, to the arguments about to be given against deductivism, that they each contain at least one premiss the truth of which could not be discovered without a mediate or immediate reliance on intuitive assessment of logical probability. No other arguments, in fact, are possible in the case, and arguments in favour of deductivism, if any could be found, would be ones which rested on no different foundation.

The following are some arguments against deductivism.

Deductivism asserts that if the argument from e to h is invalid, $P(h, e.t) = P(h, t)$. But this is false.

For (a) let h be 'Socrates is mortal'; let e be 'Socrates is a man and all of the many men observed in the past have been mortal.'

Then

(S$_1$) $P(h, e.t) < 1$,

but

(S$_2$) $P(h, e.t) \neq P(h, t)$.

Again (b) let h be 'Socrates is mortal'; let e be 'Socrates is a man born in Greece in the fifth century B.C. and 95 per cent of all men born in Greece in that century are mortal.' Then

(S$_1$) $P(h, e.t) < 1$,

but

(S$_2$) $P(h, e.t) \neq P(h, t)$.

Again (c) let h be 'Socrates is not mortal'; let e be 'Socrates is a man born in Greece in the fifth century B.C. and all men born in Greece in that century are mortal.' Then

(S$_1$) $P(h, e.t) < 1$,

but

(S$_2$) $P(h, e.t) \neq P(h, t)$.

Suppose that deductivism (6) is true. Then let there be two arguments, both invalid, from the same premiss e, to two different conclusions, h_1 and h_2. Then, by the hypothesis, $P(h_1, e.t) = P(h_1, t)$ and $P(h_2, e.t) = P(h_2, t)$, and by the symmetry of irrelevance (in Keynes's sense),[7] $P(e, h_1.t) = P(e, t) = P(e, h_2.t)$. Thus deductivism entails that if both of two arguments from the same premiss to different conclusions are invalid, the corresponding 'inverse' arguments have the same logical probability. But this is false.

For (d) let e be '5 per cent of the present Australian bird population are white'; let h_1 be '5 per cent of the many observed Australian birds are white'; and let h_2 be '95 per cent of the many observed Australian birds are white.' Then

(S$_1$) $P(h_1, e) < 1$,

and

(S$_2$) $P(h_2, e) < 1$,

but

(S$_3$) $P(e, h_1) \neq P(e, h_2)$.

[7] i.e. by the principle of logical probability that if $P(q, r.p) = P(q, r)$ then $P(p, r.q) = P(p, r)$ (provided q and r are consistent).

Again (e) let e be '5 per cent of the many observed Australian birds are white'; let h_1 be '5 per cent of the present Australian bird population are white'; and let h_2 be '95 per cent of the present Australian bird population are white.' Then

(S$_1$) $P(h_1, e) < 1$,

and

(S$_2$) $P(h_2, e) < 1$,

but

(S$_3$) $P(e, h_1) \neq P(e, h_2)$.

Again (f) let e be 'All Australian native swans alive at present are white'; let h_1 be 'Some Australian native birds alive at present are white and not swans'; and let h_2 be 'Some Australian native swans alive at present are not white.' Then

(S$_1$) $P(h_1, e) < 1$,

and

(S$_2$) $P(h_2, e) < 1$,

but

(S$_3$) $P(e, h_1) \neq P(e, h_2)$.

Objection is very likely to be made to the arguments (a) and (d) along the following lines: that these arguments have among their premises some of the natural favourable assessments of certain inductive inferences, and that consequently they beg the question against deductivism.

But we saw in section (i) above that the sceptical assessment of induction (8) is not part of the content of deductivism (6). Consequently, to assert such contraries of inductive scepticism (8) as the proposition (S$_2$) in argument (a), or the proposition (S$_3$) in (d), is not to deny any part of what deductivism (6) affirms. These propositions would indeed beg the question, if they were advanced as premises of an argument against inductive scepticism. But in the present chapter the thesis which is in question is not inductive scepticism but the logically independent one of deductivism. So the inference of my imaginary objector is invalid.

His premise is also false. It is not true that (S$_2$) in argument (a), or (S$_3$) in (d), asserts the natural favourable assessment of a certain inductive inference. For neither of these two propositions says which of the two arguments mentioned in it has the greater logical

Some arguments against deductivism

probability. Each merely denies, what deductivism conjoined with the preceding judgements of invalidity entails, that their logical probabilities are equal. In other words, the premisses of the two arguments (a) and (d) are entirely consistent with the *un*natural (counter-inductive) assessment, $P(h, e.t) < P(h, t)$ in connection with (a), or $P(e, h_1) < P(e, h_2)$ in connection with (d).

To our imaginary objector we may reply, therefore, that arguments (a) and (d) would not beg the question against deductivism even if their premisses did include some of the natural favourable assessments of certain inductive inferences; but that in fact they do not.

What is of course true, and all the truth that lies behind the objection just answered, is that arguments (a) and (d) ought not to be regarded as the reduction of deductivism to absurdity by a deductivist who is also an inductive sceptic. Against such a deductivist (Hume for example), one would have to rely on arguments other than (a) and (d): for example, on the arguments (b), (c), (e), and (f) above. But (a) and (d) are not on this account any the worse as arguments against deductivism: which is what they are here offered as being. And it would be idle, of course, to try to construct any argument which would be at once a *reductio ad absurdum* of a thesis T, and recognizable as such by every adherent of T regardless of what other thesis T′ he might happen also to maintain.

It will be evident that the arguments given above against deductivism could easily be added to. For the arguments (a)–(f) all concern one or other of just three kinds of invalid inference: inductive inference, Bernoullian inference, and inferences which are not only invalid but have a conclusion actually inconsistent with their premiss. Even within this limited range, all the arguments given are from *singular* statements of logical probability only, and are therefore only a small fragment of the arguments against deductivism which naturally arise from a consideration of even the above three kinds of invalid inference. There would be little point, however, in adding other arguments of this kind, since their premisses would be likely to meet with acceptance where and only where the premisses of the arguments already given do so.

There is, however, one other argument against deductivism which it will be worthwhile to add, because its premisses are sufficiently different from those of any of the arguments (a)–(f). This is an adaptation of the argument of von Thun against inductive scepticism.

We affirm two judgements of regularity, $P(Fa, t) < 1$ and $P(\sim Fb \vee \sim Fa, t) < 1$, as well as certain obvious judgements of validity mentioned in the preceding chapter, note 5. These of course are simply the premisses of the von Thun argument, and from them follows the falsity of inductive scepticism (8). But inductive scepticism is a consequence, as Hume argued, of deductivism (6), conjoined with the fallibilist premiss that for all inductive arguments e to h, $P(h, e.t) < 1$. Hence we need only further affirm this inductive-fallibilist thesis, and the falsity of Hume's other premiss, deductivism, follows.

The arguments given above, despite their being only a small selection from those available, suffice to do what any number of arguments against deductivism would in the end have to be content with doing. For deductivism (6) is so comprehensive and undiscriminating an unfavourable assessment of invalid inferences, that all that arguments against it can do is this: to 'assemble reminders', (in Wittgenstein's phrase), of the number and variety of statements of logical probability, of which the truth is intuitively obvious, which would all have to be denied if deductivism were admitted. The arguments given disclose only a corner of this field; but they will serve to suggest how immense a field it is.

Even so, the group of arguments (a)–(f) is diversified enough to show that the sceptical consequences of accepting deductivism are not at all confined to inductive inference. They show that, on the contrary, deductivism, conjoined with appropriate and true judgements of invalidity, entails sceptical equalities concerning even the most conclusive of statistical inferences, and even concerning inferences some of which have, while others have not, conclusions inconsistent with their premisses. And while the arguments (a)–(f) point out that deductivism generates not only inductive but statistical and other scepticisms, the argument adapted from von Thun points out that deductivism at the same time generates the extreme *credulity* of denying either inductive fallibilism (9) or else one of the judgements of regularity (S_1) or (S_2) of Chapter 5 section (*iii*).

The balance of arguments concerning deductivism, therefore, is this. We have indefinitely many, and various, reasons, each one of them in itself sufficient, for thinking that it is false. And to be set against these, the reasons we have for thinking it true are—non-existent.

If deductivism is false, we saw in section (*i*) above, then the fundamental thesis of the theory of logical probability is true. Any

Some arguments against deductivism

argument against deductivism is at the same time, therefore, an argument for that thesis. And in fact the great fund of natural comparative inequalities, which deductivism (as arguments (a)–(f) show) would obliterate, constitutes most of the raw materials which the theory of logical probability exists to systematize. It is this mass of natural comparative assessments of the conclusiveness of inferences which enables the 'inductive logician' in the Carnapian sense to regard with equanimity even so basic a scepticism as was expressed by Ramsey about the foundations of the theory of logical probability.

Ramsey wrote that

there really do not seem to be any such things as the probability relations [Keynes] describes. [Keynes] supposes that, at any rate in certain cases, they can be perceived; but speaking for myself I feel confident that this is not true. I do not perceive them . . . ; moreover I shrewdly suspect that others do not perceive them either, because *they are able to come to so very little agreement as to which of them relates any two given propositions*. All we appear to know about them are certain general propositions, the laws of addition and multiplication; it is as if everyone knew the laws of geometry but no one could tell whether any given object were round or square; and I find it hard to imagine how so large a body of general knowledge can be combined with so slender a stock of particular facts.[8]

This criticism of Keynes depends for what plausibility it has on one's attention being confined to numerical equalities. But once we extend our attention to the weaker kinds of statements of logical probability, and especially to comparative equalities and inequalities, then the number and variety of the assessments of logical probability which men *are* able to come to agreement about are simply overwhelming.

[8] F. P. Ramsey, *Foundations of Mathematics* (London, 1931), pp. 161–2. My italics.

7

THE TRUTH AND IMPORTANCE OF ITS FALLIBILIST CONSEQUENCE

(i) The independence of inductive scepticism and inductive fallibilism

Hume's inductive fallibilism asserts that all inductive inferences are invalid, and 'incurably' so, in the sense that they remain invalid under any observational addition to their premisses; or abbreviated, (9) '$P(h, e_1.t) < 1$ and $P(h, e_1.e_2.t) < 1$ if the argument from e_1 to h is inductive and e_2 is observational'. His inductive scepticism asserts that all inductive inferences are unreasonable, or (8) '$P(h, e.t) = P(h, t)$ if the argument from e to h is inductive'. Now, when we consider these propositions by themselves, it is obvious that neither the truth nor the falsity of inductive fallibilism requires either the truth or the falsity of inductive scepticism. The two propositions are logically independent.

This was not always obvious to Hume, since (as was remarked in Chapter 3 section *(iii)*), he sometimes treats these two very different propositions as though they were equivalent. I do not think (despite Professor Mossner's admission mentioned above) that there is any need to question Hume's honesty on this account. A certain tendency to conflate inductive fallibilism with inductive scepticism was to be expected in view of one of those conflicts of purpose in Hume which Professor Passmore has so well portrayed.[1] When he undertook to examine 'that evidence which assures us of any real existence and matter of fact',[2] Hume, it is clear, wanted to do two different things. On the one hand he wanted to stand forth as a champion of sober experimental science, against what he regarded as the parties of credulity and dogmatism. But, on the other hand, he wanted to search that topic to the bottom, as a philosopher does, applying to all inferences as he goes along the most rigorous standard of conclusiveness; and in this frame of mind a man is

[1] In his *Hume's Intentions* (Cambridge, 1952). [2] *Enquiry*, p. 26.

indifferent to the politics of the republic of letters, and in particular does not stop to consider whether his investigations will injure his own party therein. The first motive was bound to incline Hume towards inductive fallibilism; the second, towards inductive scepticism.

But more than that: consider how the two theses are logically related, when taken in conjunction with other propositions which Hume assumed. When inductive fallibilism is taken along with the deductivist thesis (6), it does entail inductive scepticism. And when inductive scepticism is taken along with the regularity thesis (4), it does entail the fallibility of inductive inference. But (4) and (6) are, as we have seen, propositions which Hume took so much for granted that, although he certainly assumed them in his argument for scepticism, he left them unstated. Nothing could be more natural, consequently, than that he should at least sometimes write as though scepticism and fallibilism about induction were the same thing.

What makes the difference between them all the more palpable to us, is that at the present time the currency of the two theses is so very different. Inductive scepticism, as I have said in Chapter 5 section (i), has acquired in the last fifty years a certain, very limited, currency; but the triumph of inductive fallibilism has been complete.

(ii) *The currency of inductive fallibilism*

To say that inductive inferences are all incurably invalid is another way of saying that there is a permanent possibility of falsity in even the best-confirmed empirical generalizations and predictions. This is certainly a belief having extremely wide currency at the present time. Philosophers, I think, almost without exception accept it; but not only they. It has been absorbed into the common-sense philosophy of science which most educated men now share. It is taken for granted by many intelligent schoolboys. This conviction, moreover, is a living one: it is believed that there is a *real* possibility that any given scientific generalization or prediction might have to be given up in the light of subsequent experience. Finally, it is a steady conviction; not one which is, as it were, put on just for certain special intellectual occasions. The currency of inductive fallibilism, in other words, is in every respect the opposite of such currency as inductive scepticism can claim to have.

Matters did not always stand so, as I will soon have occasion to emphasize. But at present the incurable invalidity of inductive inference is so well recognized that there is a tendency to make invalidity part of what is *meant* by calling an inference 'inductive'. In Carnap's usage of 'inductive', to say that inductive inferences are all invalid, is trivial in precisely the same way as 'Bachelors are all unmarried'. But (as was remarked in Chapter 1 section (*ix*)), that usage is still not the main one. In the main stream of usage, as also here, it will be recalled, 'inductive inference' has no evaluative meaning. (Here it is simply a translation of Hume's 'probable arguments', which at the relevant places in Hume's text simply means, as we saw, 'arguments from observed to unobserved instances of empirical predicates'.) On this understanding, the thesis of inductive fallibilism at any rate *could* be a non-trivial truth.

(*iii*) *Its truth*

That it is in any case true is something which can be learnt from Hume's argument for inductive scepticism. For from Hume's premisses (e), (f), and the regularity premiss (4), it follows, as we have seen, that: all inductive inferences are invalid as they stand, and the addition to their premisses which is necessary in order to turn them into valid inferences is a proposition not deducible from necessary truths, and not deducible, either, from observational premisses without such an addition to them as would make the inference to that proposition circular. And this complex result reduces, we saw in Chapter 3 section (*ii*), to the statement that all inductive inferences are invalid and remain so under observational additions to their premisses.

But, I have argued briefly in Chapter 1 section (*vi*), the regularity premiss, that there can be no demonstrative arguments for a matter of fact, or (4) '$P(h, t) < 1$ for all contingent h', is true. Likewise, I have argued briefly in Chapter 2 section (*iii*), that Hume's premiss (e) is true: that all inductive inferences are invalid as they stand and can be turned into valid ones only by the addition of the Resemblance Thesis to their premisses. For the truth of (f), 'The Resemblance Thesis is contingent', I now argue briefly as follows: from (e), in conjunction with an assumption which I have already employed in the 'reduction' referred to above. This is, that a proposition which is needed to turn an invalid argument with a contingent conclusion into a valid one, is contingent.

If these arguments are correct, then (e), (f), and (4) are all true. Then their consequence, inductive fallibilism, must also be true.

(iv) Its non-triviality: one reason why inductive fallibilism is important

Supposing inductive fallibilism true, the best way to show that it is a non-trivial truth would be to show that there is something in men which strongly disposes them to deny it, or at least to disregard it. For we would then have shown that inductive fallibilism needs to be emphasized, as a corrective to a deep-seated tendency to error. We would *a fortiori* have shown that a proof of inductive fallibilism, such as Hume provided, and as distinct from mere assertion of it, is a valuable contribution to the philosophy of science.

Is there, then, anything in us which puts us in need of a reminder of inductive fallibilism? Yes: at least if Hume is right, there are in fact two distinct sources of a powerful tendency in men to disregard the truth of inductive fallibilism.

First, *pride*—'the pride of mere human reasoners', as Hume says.[3] Or more accurately, that complex of mental traits, of which pride is merely a prominent usual component, which sometimes causes men of science to treat a certain universal generalization, say, which is confessedly grounded in the end only on observational evidence, as though no subsequent empirical evidence could possibly refute it. Presumably, other common components of that state of mind are 'the search for certainty', and ordinary intellectual unimaginativeness.

Valid inferences all have, and they alone have, the characteristic that their logical probability is unaffected under all possible additions to their premises. That is, both in the Keynesian and in the ordinary untechnical sense of 'irrelevant', e_2 is irrelevant to h relative to e_1, for all e_2, if and only if the argument from e_1 to h is valid. And it must be admitted that for a man to behave as though all observational e_2 were necessarily irrelevant to a favoured theory h—i.e. as though the argument from e_1 to h were valid—when in fact that argument is inductive, is no unheard-of occurrence in the history of science.

The mental traits which can cause such an overestimation, by a scientist, of the conclusiveness of certain inductive inferences, sometimes, moreover, triumph over all opposing tendencies among the wider body of educated men. Then an entire period of inductive over-confidence sets in. An example of such a period, and probably both the most extreme and the most important, is that roughly from 1700 to 1900: the period of the Newtonian supremacy. In order to

---

[3] In the passage quoted in Chapter 3 from the *Letter from a Gentleman*. But of course the theme is a recurrent one with Hume. Cf. e.g. *Enquiry*, pp. 161-2.

see whether inductive fallibilism is a corrective that is ever needed, it will be instructive to reflect briefly on two striking features of the intellectual climate of that period.

On the one hand, it is a distinguishing feature of the period that observation and experiment are said, repeatedly and emphatically, to be the only kind of evidence on the basis of which an empirical generalization or prediction can acquire a claim to our belief. Everything else—revelation, sacred tradition, Aristotle, universal assent, the fitness of things, inner light, pure reason—is denied all authority in empirical science, by almost every characteristic writer of the period. We, of course, have great difficulty in entering into imaginative sympathy with a state of mind in which these self-denying ordinances would require a painful effort. Yet they plainly did require that, and it can only be a deficiency in our historical imagination which inclines us to think otherwise. This fact on its own should prepare us for the possibility that we might be guilty of a similar deficiency in historical imagination, if we think that inductive fallibilism can never be a needed corrective.

On the other hand, however, a second feature of this period is that, during it, the successes of Newtonian mechanics and gravitation theory were such as to overwhelm, in almost every informed mind, any lingering doubt as to their precise and universal truth. Even very early in the eighteenth century, confidence that space, time, and matter had universally the properties which Newton attributed to them was so wide and deep as to consign the doubts even of a Leibniz and a Berkeley to a long oblivion. And by the end of that century, Kant could erect a whole philosophy just in order to explain how empirical knowledge of such universality and finality was possible. (It is part of Kant's lasting merit that he perceived that this *is* a problem; but then he had been awakened by the great inductive fallibilist.) Or consider the writer whose influence predominated in the philosophy of science in Britain in the second half of the nineteenth century. J. S. Mill insists that ultimately the evidence for scientific generalizations can only be observational. Yet he plainly also believes that observational evidence can be such, and actually has been such, as to place at least some universal generalizations, viz. at least those of Newtonian mechanics and gravitation, beyond the possibility of falsity. Mill does, indeed, write for example that 'we must hold even our strongest convictions with an opening left in our minds for the reception of facts which contradict them...'⁴ But even this is with him a maxim of the ethics of intellectual life in general, rather than specifically a concession to inductive fallibilism. It is evident to any reader of Mill that he has no *living* conviction of the possibility that subsequent experience might require changes in the Newtonian framework.

It should go without saying that these are brush-strokes of the broadest kind, and are subject to countless qualifications and corrections; even geographical ones. For example, for reasons not entirely intellectual, confidence in the finality of the Newtonian generalizations was more pronounced in Britain, on the whole, than elsewhere. But taken in the large, the philosophy of science prevailing during this period does have these two characteristics: the Baconian emphasis on the sole authority for empirical science of observational evidence, and the conviction that the Newtonian generalizations had been placed, by the evidence in their favour, beyond the reach of subsequent correction. If so, then there *are* periods, since the *pax Newtoniana* was one, when a reminder is needed of the truth of inductive fallibilism. It is, in fact, only one lifetime ago that 'the pride of mere human reasoners' last needed such a reminder.

It seems at present as though inductive fallibilism has been absorbed into the thought of educated men for good. If this really is so, then there is indeed one sense in which inductive fallibilism has become, or is becoming, trivial: the sense in which any very general, simple, logico-philosophical truth, once perceived as true by all educated men, is trivial. But that is a sense in which it is perfectly possible for a proposition to be trivial and still be one of the great intellectual conquests of the human race. Some other judgements of invalidity are in that sense, and in that sense alone, trivial yet also truths of great importance. For example, '$P(x$ is F, x is G, and all F are $G) < 1$', the invalidity of undistributed middle for logically independent predicates.

Inductive fallibilism itself, however, forbids us to repose an entire confidence in the permanence of men's belief in inductive fallibilism. It is possible, in every sense of 'possible', that the future history of science may contain further periods of inductive overconfidence. But even if it should turn out that the last fallibilist reminder ever needed was that which was administered to Newtonian over-confidence at the beginning of this century, still there is

⁴ *A System of Logic* (8th edn., London, 1843), p. 376.

something else in us which stands in need of the fallibilist reminder, and which is quite distinct from intellectual pride, and far less amenable to correction.

(v) *A second reason why it is important*

This is what, to distinguish it from the 'scientific' inductive over-confidence just discussed, may be called 'organic' inductive over-confidence. The former is occasional, and affects only the educated; the latter is (at least comparatively) permanent, deep-seated, and common to the learned and the vulgar alike. It is displayed, in particular, in the over-assessment which men, as well as some of the lower animals, make of the conclusiveness of the predictive-inductive inference. That is (to return to our stock example), of the inference from 'This is a flame, and all of the many flames observed in the past have been hot' to 'This is hot'.

Let us compare the degree of conclusiveness which it is natural to ascribe to this inference, with that which it is natural to ascribe to some other: for example, to the non-inductive inference from 'This die is about to be thrown, and is a fair die marked in the usual way', to 'This throw will not result in a "four".' Now men naturally ascribe a high degree of conclusiveness to this Bernoullian inference, as they do to the predictive-inductive one. But there is no natural tendency whatever to ascribe to it the highest possible degree of conclusiveness; i.e. to mistake it for a valid inference. On the contrary, everyone recognizes that, in relation to its premisses, its conclusion is a proper subject of betting. Everyone can easily, by introspection, discriminate between the degree of conclusiveness which he naturally ascribes to this inference, and that which he naturally ascribes to *modus ponens* or to Barbara, for example.

The same is true, of course, of many inductive inferences, but, if Hume is right, not of all; and in particular, not of the predictive-inductive inference. For with us, Hume says, that kind of inference is *'entirely free from doubt and uncertainty'*;[5] it leaves *'no room for doubt or opposition'*.[6] A man who knows the premiss of a predictive-inductive inference believes the conclusion 'with the last degree of assurance, and regards his past experience as a full *proof*'[7] of the hotness of the next flame. And surely Hume is right? In organisms such as we are, the characteristic effect of a long uniform experience

[5] *Treatise*, p. 124. My italics.   [6] *Enquiry*, p. 56 n. My italics.
[7] Ibid., p. 110. Hume's italics.

of flames as being hot, and the observation of a new flame, *is* to produce a mental state in which we cannot at all recognize 'This is hot' as a proper subject of betting. We have no *living* conviction of the possibility of the falsity of that conclusion. (This is a factual claim which any of us can test—I admit only rather roughly and not quite directly—by determining how willing we are to put a hand deliberately into the next flame we see). The degree of conclusiveness which men naturally ascribe to the predictive-inductive inference is not introspectively discriminable from that which they naturally ascribe to Barbara or *modus ponens*.

I agree with Hume, then, on the factual question as to what degree of conclusiveness men ascribe to the predictive-inductive inference. But Hume is right too on the non-factual question, as to what degree of conclusiveness that kind of inference really has; at least, qua inductive fallibilist, as distinct from inductive sceptic, he is right. For inferences of that kind are what inductive fallibilism says they are, and what Barbara and *modus ponens* are not: invalid, and consequently not of the highest possible degree of conclusiveness.

Men, therefore, are inveterate over-estimators of the conclusiveness of the predictive-inductive inference. However closely we may approach the ideal of the completely rational inferrer in connection with some inferences, including the Bernoullian inference about the die and even some inductive ones, we regularly fall short of that ideal in connection with some other inductive inferences. Inductive fallibilism, consequently, is needed as a standing reminder that even if predictive-inductive inferences are more conclusive than Hume's inductive scepticism says they are, still they are less conclusive than all of us every day take them to be.

If there were no inductive over-confidence, either scientific or organic, then indeed inductive fallibilism, though true, would not be a truth we needed to be reminded of, or even taught at all; there would be nothing in us for inductive fallibilism to 'bite on', as it were. But there is inductive over-confidence, both scientific and organic, and, in consequence, inductive fallibilism is important, as well as true; and a proof of it, such as Hume's, is therefore a proof of an important truth.

8

OUR HISTORICAL DEBTS TO HUME'S ARGUMENT FOR SCEPTICISM

(i) Twentieth-century inductive fallibilism

The most that follows, I have tried to show, from the true premisses of Hume's argument for inductive scepticism, is the incurable invalidity of all inductive inferences. Inductive fallibilism (9) therefore, if I am right, exhausts Hume's positive contribution to the philosophy of induction. In the present century, when Hume's reputation has been raised to an immense height, far above where it stood for nearly two centuries, many writers have credited him with contributions to the philosophy of induction which go far beyond this. If my account of Hume's argument is correct, all these claims must be erroneous;[1] and it is interesting to observe, as one frequently can do in conversation with contemporary philosophers, that when Hume is claimed to have proved some important thesis about inductive inference, the thesis almost always contracts, under pressure, to one of non-deducibility, i.e. to inductive fallibilism.[2]

If, however, we consider the historical effects of Hume's argument for inductive scepticism, then it will appear that our intellectual debts to it are much greater than they would seem to have been just from what was said in the preceding chapter about the importance of inductive fallibilism.

At the present time, as I have already said, inductive fallibilism has become a commonplace. But less than 100 years ago, it was not only not so, but rather the contradictory thesis was a commonplace, if anything. Thus the author of a manual of 'inductive logic' belonging to the predominant school of Mill writes in 1876 that 'we

---

[1] Some of the more extravagant claims made on Hume's behalf, by writers during the last fifty years, are collected and briefly discussed in the Appendix section *(iii)*.

[2] Theses of non-deducibility, i.e. judgements of invalidity, can fairly be said to have been Hume's *forte* in general. In ethics, for example, the most important proposition which is associated with his name is '$P(h, e) < 1$ for all factual e and ethical h'.

can hardly conceive men of science commonly speaking of the most firmly established generalisations of mechanics, optics, or chemistry, simply as conclusions possessing a high degree of probability.'[3] Nor is this an exceptional remark: Fowler certainly speaks for the prevailing philosophy of science, and for the educated common sense, of his time. Even Hume himself, as we have seen, admits that 'one would appear ridiculous who would say, that 'tis only probable the sun will rise to-morrow, or that all men must die; tho' 'tis plain we have no further assurance of these facts, than what experience affords us.'[4] Because ''tis . . . certain, that in common discourse we readily affirm, that many arguments from causation exceed probability, and may be received as a superior kind of evidence.'

It will hardly need to be emphasized that what Fowler found hardly conceivable is now so much a commonplace that it is the opposite which is difficult to conceive; and that what Hume was sure would 'appear ridiculous' to his contemporaries does not appear so at all to ours. With us, in fact, as the titles of innumerable books and articles testify, the difficulty is to mention induction *without* mentioning probability in the same breath. There has been, then, in the last 100 years, a remarkable conversion to belief in the thesis of inductive fallibilism. What brought it about? Inductive fallibilism, as I have said, could be learnt, at any time, from Hume's argument for inductive scepticism. But from what, at this time, has it been learnt, as a matter of historical fact?

With a partial exception to be mentioned later, it is from philosophers that inductive fallibilism is learnt, both by philosophers and by others. And a philosopher at the present time is most likely to have learnt inductive fallibilism from his own reading of Hume, and from Hume's argument for inductive scepticism in particular.[5] Consequently, one could answer the historical question posed above, by saying that Hume's argument for inductive scepticism is the source of twentieth-century inductive fallibilism; and that answer would be true. Yet it would also be very strongly suggestive of something that is not true. For Hume's argument about induction

[3] T. Fowler, *The Elements of Inductive Logic* (Oxford), preface to the third edition, p. xiii. This work 'designed mainly for the use of students in the universities' (subtitle), pretends to no originality or to any other high intellectual distinction. But of course not its quality, only its representative character, is what concerns us here.

[4] Both this and the following quoted sentence are from the long paragraph on p. 124 of the *Treatise* which was quoted in full in Chapter 2 section (*iii*) above.

[5] Along with Hume's variants of this argument. Cf. Appendix section (i).

was very far from having this effect either immediately or by a direct channel of influence. Indeed, quite generally, Hume's positive influence on the philosophy of science during the eighteenth and nineteenth centuries was extremely limited. His inductive scepticism, as has already been said, attracted no adherents, and scarcely even any notice, during that time. Even his inductive fallibilism made little lasting headway against the prevailing Newtonian over-confidence. This, and the *odium theologicum* under which all his philosophy laboured, combined to hold Hume's influence and reputation far below what they should have been; especially in England, where both of these factors operated more strongly than elsewhere. Now, however, no reputation stands higher, and Hume looms over the philosophy of induction like a colossus. Inductive fallibilism, in particular, prevails all round us. By what *indirect* channels, then, has it reached us?

There appear to be two main channels to be distinguished. Especially in the second half of the eighteenth century, Hume was a powerful influence on the general intellectual life of France, and one place where his inductive fallibilism, in particular, undoubtedly struck root, was among the writers on probability in that country around 1800 and shortly thereafter. Hume is sometimes supposed to have been a critic—even, by Keynes, for example, an 'effective'[6] critic—of the 'classical' theorists of probability. This supposition I believe to be groundless,[7] but if he was, his criticisms completely escaped their notice. His inductive scepticism, of course, met the same disbelief there as everywhere else. His inductive fallibilism, on the other hand, was welcome and important to the probability theorists; and it is not hard to see why.

Up to the middle of the eighteenth century, the classical theory of probability had remained almost entirely embedded in the consideration of games of chance.[8] That is to say, while the *principles* of probability could be, and often were, detached from that limited context, and stated quite generally; and the auxiliary mathematics to which the theory had given rise, for example the algebra of combinations, also could be, and often was, stated without even any mention of probability, as it should be; still it was almost always from 'problems in play' that the *statements* of probability, in

---

[6] *A Treatise on Probability*, p. 83.   [7] Cf. Appendix sections (*ii*) and (*iii*).
[8] Certainly up to the third edition, in 1756, of de Moivre's *Doctrine of Chances, or a method of calculating the probabilities of events in play*.

particular the numerical assessments of particular probabilities, were drawn, and applications provided for the principles. According to inductive fallibilism, however, the non-demonstrative character possessed by most of the inferences which men make in connection with games of chance is shared by all those inferences which men make from the observed to the unobserved in empirical science. If that is true, games of chance, from being almost the whole of the area of application of the theory of probability, become only a small and comparatively unimportant part of that area.

Among the theorists of probability, where the influence of Hume's writings about inductive inference was strong, but his scepticism rejected, one would expect, therefore, that inductive fallibilism would be seen as offering an enormous acquisition of new territory: as bringing within the area of application of the principles, and the mathematics, of probability nothing less than the whole of empirical science. In particular one would expect inductive fallibilism to bestow a novel importance on 'Bayes's Theorem', or Laplace's 'Sixth Principle'[9] of probability: that principle which was described as enabling us, given the '*a priori*' probability of a certain causal hypothesis and the 'direct' probability of certain observations relative to that hypothesis, to deduce the 'inverse' probability of that causal hypothesis relative to those observations. The direct probabilities, of course, would be supplied by the 'Theorems' of Bernoulli.

And that, of course, is precisely what did happen. It was the novel claim of the school of Laplace, in the last quarter of the eighteenth century and the first quarter of the nineteenth, that, as Laplace himself writes in the famous *Essai*, 'the entire system of human knowledge'[10] belongs to the province of the theory of probability. Accordingly, as historians of the theory of probability have remarked, there is hardly any inference, inductive or otherwise, the probability of which the writers of this period seem to have thought it beyond the powers of the inverse principle, and Bernoulli's Theorems, to assess.[11] The often-quoted *dictum* of Quetelet is the confident epitome of this great expansion of claims made on behalf of the theory of probability: 'L'urne que nous interrogeons, c'est la

[9] *Essai philosophique sur les probabilités* (Paris, 1814), Ch. III.
[10] *A Philosophical Essay on Probabilities*, trans. Truescott and Emory (Dover, N.Y., 1951), p. 2.
[11] Cf. Keynes, *Treatise*, Chs. VII, XVIII, XXX; Todhunter, *History of the Mathematical Theory of Probability* (Cambridge, 1865), Chs. XVI–XX.

nature.'[12] It will be evident that that *dictum* would simply not be possible except where the prevailing philosophy of science contained, as an absolutely settled tenet, inductive fallibilism.

And it was Hume who furnished the Laplacean school with its philosophy of science. This fact has been remarked upon by other writers, for example von Wright.[13] Nor were the writers of this school themselves backward in acknowledging their debts to Hume; as can be seen from such a manual of the classical theory of probability as that of Lacroix, first published in 1816.[14] Less than half of this book is occupied with the problems in play which were the staple of the older theory of probability, and all the rest of it bears the impress, constantly acknowledged, of Hume's philosophy of induction (without, of course, his scepticism). This section of the book takes in the whole field of inductive inference under the heading of 'Détermination de la probabilité des causes (ou des hypothèses) par les observations':[15] which determination, Lacroix believes, can in every case be made by Bayes's principle with the aid of Bernoulli's Theorems. The probabilities which these together yield will preserve us, on the one side, from Hume's inductive scepticism; and, on the other, from that dogmatism and inductive over-confidence which is 'infiniment plus dangereuse que la première',[16] because we are inclined to it both by reactionary philosophies[17] and by our natural habits of mind.[18] The theory of probability thus provides 'un moyen très spécieux de réfuter les excès du scepticisme, sans recourir à ces principes posés *a priori* . . .';[19] a 'doctrine moyenne, que l'on pourrait nommer *scepticisme gradué* . . .'[20]

The school of Laplace, then, taking their philosophy of science from Hume, claimed the whole field of inductive inference for the theory of probability. But that means that, for them, the fundamental thing to be learnt from Hume was the discovery that inductive inferences even at the best resemble, in their degrees of conclusiveness, the kind of inference which is characteristic, not of mathematics or logic, but of games of chance.

---

[12] Quoted, e.g. by Keynes, *Treatise*, p. 428. But I am unable to say where Quetelet wrote this.
[13] Cf. *The Logical Problem of Induction* (2nd edn., London, 1957), p. 220 n. 1.
[14] S. F. Lacroix, *Traité élémentaire du calcul des probabilités*. (My page-references are to the 3rd edn., Paris, 1833.)
[15] Ibid. p. 172. [16] Ibid. p. 181. [17] Ibid.
[18] Ibid. pp. 62–3, 181, 185. [19] Ibid. p. 299.
[20] Ibid. p. 181. Lacroix's italics.

Inductive fallibilism returned, from the theory of probability to the arena of general philosophy, and also from France to England, in a series of waves; all minor, but each a little more insistent than the one before it. It is prominent, as part of an expressly Laplacean philosophy of science, in various writings of Sir John Herschel on probability in the 1850s and 1860s;[21] in W. S. Jevons's *Principles of Science* of 1874; and in Karl Pearson's *Grammar of Science* of 1892.[22] In England it collided with the predominant philosophy of science of the J. S. Mill type, and it was in fact against the inductive fallibilism of Jevons that Fowler was vehemently protesting in the preface from which I quoted above. It is via a Laplace–Jevons channel, then, that inductive fallibilism came to be a definite element, though a subordinate one, in the philosophy of science which was current in the last quarter of the nineteenth century.

There is, however, a second and more important channel by which inductive fallibilism has reached us. Most philosophers now, as I have said, learn inductive fallibilism from Hume himself; but that in turn is possible only because of the influence on us of former members or near-members of the Vienna Circle. It is the Logical Positivist irruption into twentieth-century philosophy which has raised to their present pitch the reputation and influence of Hume's philosophy of science.

Now, in its turn, the inductive fallibilism of the Logical Positivists was no doubt derived in large part from Hume himself, perhaps partly via Mach. But it was not altogether so derived. A proof of a judgement of invalidity—that is, of the *possibility* of the premiss of an argument being true and its conclusion false—is one thing when it is from premisses purely *a priori*: and that is what Hume provided, concerning inductive arguments. But for bringing a judgement of invalidity home to men's bosoms, there is nothing so effective as a proof of it by an actual counter-example, or what is taken to be such; a case, that is, of the class of arguments in question, in which the premiss *is* true and the conclusion false. Now, for men of

[21] e.g., the article on Quetelet in the *Edinburgh Review*, 1850. (This article is sometimes erroneously attributed to the father, Sir William Herschel. All of the articles on probability attributed to that writer by Keynes (*Treatise*, p. 445), for example, are chronologically impossible. William Herschel died in 1822.)

[22] I neglect, as marginally related to the philosophy of science, though in different degrees, the influence of Laplace on such disparate thinkers as Augustus de Morgan and Francis Galton. A reminder is perhaps also needed, when one mentions such a book as Pearson's, that as with Fowler on the other side of the question of inductive fallibilism, quality of thought is not in question, only historical fact.

the circle of Carnap, Popper, and Wittgenstein, the latter was what Einstein provided. For Einstein satisfied them, as well as most others competent to judge, that some of the Newtonian generalizations were false in fact, notwithstanding the truth of all the previous empirical evidence in their favour; thus giving to philosophers and scientists a reminder, of the most striking kind, of the fallibility of even the best-confirmed of scientific generalizations.

It might seem, then, that we ought to say that at least half of the present currency of inductive fallibilism is owing, not to the influence of Hume's philosophy, but to the influence of Einstein's science (and, of course, of the continuing turbulent state of physics since 1905). And so we ought, were it not for the fact that Einstein himself several times tells us that it was Hume (and Mach, but in respect of original thought that means Hume), who woke him from his dogmatic slumbers; who taught him that no scientific generalization can be, and in particular that the absolute character attributed by Newton to time is not, necessitated by any empirical evidence.[23]

This is probably the more important channel. What the other (Laplace–Jevons) channel contributed, in net effect, was just that inductive fallibilism was a thesis of some currency in the philosophy of science *before* the world was astonished by the fall of the Newtonian empire. It merely ensured that then, when men looked around, as they will always do in a time of intellectual crisis, for something in the philosophy of science which can afford some consolation after the event, and which would even have prepared them for the event if they had adopted it in advance, they found it ready to their hand, in a general inductive fallibilism.

Thus, if there is nowadays—and there is—a cooling jet of inductive fallibilism which plays constantly on scientific confidence, preventing it from overheating, that jet has reached us by two main channels. Both are indirect, and both traverse more European than British territory. But both take their rise in Hume's argument for inductive scepticism. That argument, therefore, as well as being a permanent potential check to scientific inductive over-confidence, can fairly be said to have actually administered the fallibilist corrective which, as a matter of historical fact, Newtonian over-confidence received near the beginning of this century.

---

[23] Cf. e.g. *Albert Einstein: Philosopher-Scientist*, ed. Schilpp (Harper Torchbook edn., New York, 1959), i. 53.

It is worth observing, as a consequence, that in one respect Hume's philosophy of induction has acted in its own despite. For Hume thought that the inductive confidence of men could not be destroyed, or even weakened, by philosophical argument; but history, if my account has been correct, attests that Hume's argument for inductive scepticism *has* weakened scientific inductive confidence. It has not weakened it, of course, to the point of inductive scepticism; nor has it weakened organic inductive confidence at all, even to the point of fallibilism. But considering how recent, complete, and widespread, is the conversion to inductive fallibilism which that argument has effected, some apology is due to D. C. Williams, for the derision which greeted his suggestion, in 1947,[24] that inductive scepticism could conceivably spread from the philosopher's study to become a popular, and even a political, force.

When a truth becomes very well and widely recognized, there is always at least some tendency to trivialize it, by incorporating the predicate of it into the very meaning of the words which denote its subject. In the last thirty years this tendency has become quite pronounced in connection with inductive fallibilism, and this is what prevents the word 'inductive', or any other translation of Hume's 'probable', applied to arguments, from being a completely satisfactory translation at the present time. The tendency has, as I have earlier remarked, been carried to its conclusion in Carnap's usage of 'inductive', and we will shortly meet with an even more remarkable instance of the pressure of inductive fallibilism on our language. It is somewhat ironic to reflect that Hume, as we have seen, apologized for having, in the bulk of Book I Part III of the *Treatise*, called 'probable' certain arguments which, although they are confessedly from observed to unobserved instances, are 'in common discourse' allowed to 'exceed probability, and . . . receiv'd as a superior kind of evidence'. Ironic, because Hume's inductive fallibilism has triumphed so completely over 'common discourse', that to say ''tis only probable the sun will rise to-morrow, or that all men must die', has now become (just *because* 'we have no further assurance of these facts, than what experience affords us'), not only not 'ridiculous', but a commonplace, and is even in a fair way to being made a triviality!

[24] In *The Ground of Induction*, pp. 15-20.

(ii) Twentieth-century theory of logical probability

Hume's argument was in essence from inductive fallibilism (9) and deductivism (6), to inductive scepticism (8); and that argument is valid because, although any one of these propositions is consistent with the negation of another, the first two of them are inconsistent with the negation of the third.

For the same reason, inductive fallibilism conjoined with the denial of inductive scepticism, requires the denial of deductivism. Now, I have tried in this and the two preceding chapters to show the following: that Hume's inductive scepticism has always been, and with minor exceptions still is, denied, while his inductive fallibilism has met with wide and deep acceptance during, though not before, the twentieth century. That being so, consistency requires the denial of deductivism. But the denial of deductivism entails (as we saw in Chapter 6 section (*i*)) that sometimes two arguments, though both invalid, are of different degrees of conclusiveness; which is the fundamental thesis of the twentieth-century theory of logical probability. If, therefore, our philosophical beliefs were consistent, the currency in the twentieth century of inductive fallibilism, combined with the almost equally widespread rejection of inductive scepticism, would have been bound to bring into being, and even into prominence, the theory of logical probability.

And that, of course, is precisely what has happened. The process of adjusting our philosophy towards consistency has been slow and confused, and is still, as we saw in Chapter 6 section (*ii*), very far indeed from being complete. But the theory of logical probability did come into being just when inductive fallibilism first struck wide and deep root among philosophers and scientists, viz. in the first quarter of this century. Its development has gone on *pari passu* with the entrenchment of inductive fallibilism. And that development has been chiefly at the hands of some of the most consciously Humean of all inductive fallibilists, viz. the Logical Positivists. All of which is exactly what was to be expected from men who are unwilling to accept inductive scepticism, who are for the first time compelled to embrace inductive fallibilism in earnest, and who wish to make their philosophy of science consistent.

But this means that, in a historical sense, the twentieth-century theory of logical probability itself is something we owe to the influence of Hume's argument for inductive scepticism. This effect, to say the least, was not one which Hume intended; yet undoubtedly he produced it. He compelled us to separate the concepts of the reasonableness, and the validity, of an argument, by pointing out in the clearest manner possible the intolerable sceptical cost, in the case of inductive arguments, of not doing so. He laid down his intellectual life, so to speak, for deductivism, in order that the theory of logical probability might live. Hume ought therefore to be regarded as the patron saint of the twentieth-century theory of logical probability.

It should not be thought this piece of homage to Hume's argument for scepticism is a contrived or hypocritical one. On the contrary, the effect which I have just described his argument as having in the present century is not even the first effect of the kind which that argument has had. Early in the nineteenth century in France, as we have seen, Hume *was* honoured, because, qua inductive fallibilist, he was the conqueror of new worlds for the classical theory of probability. It is essentially the same causal sequence which has been re-enacted, only in the wider arena of general philosophy, early in the twentieth century; and the school of Carnap ought not to be more backward, in acknowledging their debt to Hume's argument for inductive scepticism, than was the school of Laplace.

(iii) On an improper way of liquidating these debts

If we consider the argument, 'No one in New York is able to cure every illness in less than two minutes, all physicians are able to do so, so, there are no physicians in New York', we may well agree with what Professor Paul Edwards says about it in a well-known article.[25] Which is, that its 'sceptical' conclusion is deduced from one premiss (the first) which is a truth everyone knows, and a second which everyone knows to be false. Or rather, if the word 'physician' is used in its ordinary sense in 'All physicians are able to cure every illness in less than two minutes', that premiss is obviously false. If not, that premiss is true, but only in the sense that a stipulative definition, however arbitrary, is true; in that case the second premiss is just an idiosyncratic 'high re-definition'[26] of the word 'physician'. For there are certainly two concepts—'physician' in the ordinary sense, and this concept with the additional requirement of being able to cure every illness in under two minutes—

---

[25] 'Bertrand Russell's Doubts About Induction', reprinted in *Logic and Language* (First Series), ed. Flew (Blackwell, Oxford, 1952).
[26] Ibid. p. 60.

which no user of ordinary English is likely to confound; but which are confounded by someone who thinks that, by arguing as above, he refutes the common-sense belief in the existence of physicians in New York.

Now, suppose it were suggested that Hume's argument, 'All inductive inferences are invalid, all invalid inferences are unreasonable, so, all inductive inferences are unreasonable', is open to the same objections. The suggestion would be that its sceptical conclusion, too, is deduced from premisses, the first of which (i.e., inductive fallibilism) is a truth that everyone knows; and the second of which (i.e., deductivism) everyone knows to be false. Or at least (it would be said), deductivism is obviously false if the words 'reasonable inference' occur in it in their ordinary sense. If they do not, then deductivism is simply an idiosyncratic high re-definition of 'reasonable inference'. For (the suggestion would run) there certainly are two concepts—'reasonable inference' in its ordinary sense, and this concept with the additional requirement of being valid—which no user of ordinary English is likely to confound; but which are confounded by someone who thinks that, by arguing as Hume did, he refutes the common-sense belief in the reasonableness of inductive inference.

It will be evident that this suggestion, if what I have said in this chapter and the two preceding ones is true, offers us a new way to pay old debts, and one with the well-known advantages which theft has over honest toil. But the suggested comparison between the two arguments would fail at every point.

Inductive fallibilism is so far from being a truth which everyone knows, that it is a truth which, at the 'organic' level, *no one* knows. And even at the level of high scientific culture, the full recognition that scientific inference, like gambling and unlike the arguments in Euclid, contains an ineradicable element of risk, has been only a very late comer into consciousness.

Deductivism is *not* an idiosyncratic high re-definition of 'reasonable inference'. It is a logico-philosophical thesis; and one of long, wide, and deep currency, at least among philosophers; which is still the unstated assumption behind much assessment of the conclusiveness of inferences, both by philosophers and by others; and which to this day has been expressly denied by almost no philosopher.

Still further from the truth, and even scandalous, would be the suggestion that the truth of inductive fallibilism, and the falsity of deductivism, are known to every one just in virtue of a command of ordinary language. Ordinary English does equip its users with two palpably distinct concepts, 'physician', and 'physician able to cure every illness in less than two minutes'; but it simply is not true that it also equips its users with two palpably distinct concepts, 'reasonable inference' and 'valid inference'.

It is indeed true, as Edwards says, that 'part of the definition of "inductive inference" is inference from something observed to something unobserved'. But it does not follow from that, as Edwards says it does, and it is not true, that 'it is a *contradiction* to say that an inference is both inductive and at the same time . . . deductively conclusive'.[27] That conclusion no more follows from that premiss, than it follows from an inference's being from the singular to the non-singular, say, or from the contingent to the non-contingent, that it cannot also be valid. To suppose that it does follow, is simply to testify to one's confidence in the truth of another premiss, which is needed to make it follow, but which as we have seen is by no means a trivial one, viz. inductive fallibilism. We see in Edwards, therefore, an instance even more remarkable than that which Carnap furnishes, of the tendency to mistake the truth of inductive fallibilism, for the recognition of which we are chiefly indebted to Hume's philosophy, for a trivial transcript of part of the meaning of the word 'inductive'.

The extent (which is great) to which inductive fallibilism is known now to be true; the extent (which is much less) to which deductivism is now known to be false; and the extent (which is still small) to which these truths have become incorporated in ordinary language: *all* these, if what I have said is true, are due to the influence of Hume's argument for inductive scepticism. If, therefore, someone were to suggest that that argument is open to the same objections as the above sceptical argument about the physicians, the situation would be as follows. That the man who taught everyone to see empirical science as incurably fallible, would be being blamed for affirming a truth which every one knew before, and knew in virtue of a mere command of ordinary language; and that the man who compelled us to separate the two concepts of 'valid' and of 'reasonable inference', would be being reproached for neglecting this distinction which every user of ordinary English is alleged to be conscious of. We should have the exquisite irony that the effects of Hume's philosophical triumph over 'common discourse' would be being

[27] This and the preceding quotation, ibid. pp. 68–9. Edwards's italics.

mistaken for wisdom which ordinary language itself gives *gratis* to all its users. It would be a scandalous repudiation of debts fairly contracted, if a philosopher were to compare Hume's argument with that about the physicians.

It was with an argument of Russell, not of Hume, that Edwards compared the argument about the physicians. He therefore may not be exposed to the reproaches I have conditionally made. Writing when he was, Russell should perhaps not have made, as he did, the deductivist assumption. Yet it comes as something of a shock to be reminded that Edwards was writing, in 1949, about a book published in 1912. That date was distinctly before the full tide of inductive fallibilism had arrived even at Cambridge: a fact of which anyone can satisfy himself by reading the opening pages of the first of Broad's famous articles of 1918 on 'The Relation between Induction and Probability'.[28] One is entitled to wonder, then, whether Edwards's treatment of Russell was much less unfair than it would have been if applied to Hume. In any case, as Edwards was of course well aware, Russell was simply repeating the essentials of Hume's argument for inductive scepticism. Besides which, Edwards's article confessedly was just one application of a *general* method for liquidating debts which might be supposed to be owing to great philosophers, by portraying their relation to ordinary language as almost exclusively that of parasite to host. There are grounds, then, for thinking that Edwards did intend to compare the argument about the physicians with Hume's argument about induction; and if so, then what was said conditionally above does apply to him.

[28] *Mind*, vol. 27.

9

CONCLUDING REMARKS

'Hitherto Hume has been master, only to be refuted in the manner of Diogenes and Dr. Johnson.' So, as we saw in the Introduction, wrote Keynes in 1921.[1] In the preceding pages, refutations have been offered both of Hume's conclusion about induction and of one of the premisses from which he inferred that conclusion. By their extreme simplicity, as well as some of their other features, these attempted refutations are likely to excite a suspicion that in this book, too, Hume has been 'refuted' only after the manner of Diogenes and Dr. Johnson.

If, however, Keynes meant by that 'manner', what he is most likely to have meant by it, this suspicion is certainly false. For Keynes presumably meant to refer to a kind of attempted refutation of philosophical paradoxes, which consists in the (essentially wordless) performance of certain familiar actions. If so, the Johnsonian manner of 'refuting' Hume's inductive scepticism would consist, presumably, in one's simply *making*, or continuing to make, inductive inferences. But it will not require emphasis that that is not what has been done in this book.

Alternatively, 'refutation' in the Johnsonian manner might be taken to consist in meeting a philosopher's startling conclusion with a mere emphatic assertion of its falsity. But on this interpretation, too, my attempted refutations are not after the manner of Johnson. For I have not contented myself with asserting, but have endeavoured to prove, the falsity of Hume's sceptical conclusion and of his deductivist premiss.

If, again, Johnsonian 'refutation' of a philosopher's sceptical theses is taken to consist in the advancing of question-begging arguments against them, then my attempted refutations are still free from the reproach of being Johnsonian. My arguments against

---

[1] See Introduction, p. 2 above.

deductivism contained no question-begging, even at the only places where they might appear to do so, viz. at the arguments (a) and (d) in Chapter 6 section (*iv*). For those two arguments, we saw, do not rest on the favourable assessment which it is natural to make of certain inductive inferences, and would not be question-begging even if they did. Then, in von Thun's argument against inductive scepticism, so far from there being any question begged against Hume, the premisses could in fact have been deduced from a thesis which is actually embraced quite clearly by Hume himself (viz. the Regularity premiss (4)).

But the suspicion that my attempted refutations of Hume are in *some* sense too easy to be effective, will not be easily dispelled. After all, statements of logical probability, even proved ones, are mere 'analytic' propositions (as it is often put, and as I have been at pains to emphasize, though in different words). Such insubstantial weapons, it will be thought, cannot inflict much injury on the diamond-hard body of Hume's philosophy of induction.

This thought, however, rests on a fundamental misconception of the nature of Hume's sceptical conclusion, a misconception which it was an essential part of the purpose of Chapters 2–4 to correct. For if it is supposed that proof of mere analytic propositions could not refute Hume's conclusion, that can only be because it is supposed that that conclusion itself is not another proposition of the same kind, but is, rather, a factual one. Yet, that this cannot be so, ought to have been evident both on textual and on philosophical grounds. On textual grounds, because Hume's only argument for his scepticism turns out, on identification, to have been a valid one from premisses none of which are factual. On philosophical grounds, because Hume's sceptical conclusion is certainly universal (it concerns *all* inductive inferences); and hence it would, if it were also factual, be just one of the propositions (such as 'All flames are hot') which it itself says we can have 'no reason' to believe.

This point, the non-factual character of Hume's inductive scepticism, is the key to everything else in this book, and in particular to the present question, of the sufficiency of the kind of argument advanced in Chapter 5 for the falsity of that scepticism. If, indeed, Hume's inductive scepticism were a proposition about the relative frequency with which inductive inferences from true premisses have true conclusions, then no proof of a statement of logical probability could be equal to the task of refuting it. But it is not, and could not be, such a proposition. Any argument against it is bound, on the contrary, to be of the same general character as Hume's argument for it, viz. uniformly non-factual throughout. von Thun's argument is such, and even, as it happens, exactly resembles Hume's argument for inductive scepticism, in resting on two judgements of invalidity. (Hume's two are inductive fallibilism (9), and the regularity premiss (4); von Thun's are the judgements of regularity (S1) and (S2) of Chapter 5 section (*iii*).)

It is especially absurd at the present time to suppose, in effect, that Hume's inductive scepticism is a factual proposition. For, as has been remarked earlier, it is now quite often supposed, as it never was before the twentieth century, that Hume really did *prove* his sceptical conclusion about induction; which makes the absurdity of the former supposition greater than it would have been before the present century. Yet both suppositions are made, in effect, by some contemporary philosophers, as will shortly be shown. This absurdity issues, moreover, in an attitude to critics of Hume which amounts to one of 'Heads Hume wins, tails his critic loses'. For the critic of Hume's inductive scepticism is debarred, on the one hand, from using as his premisses propositions of a general factual kind (concerning the uniformity of nature, say, or the long-run success rate of inductive inferences). He is properly so debarred, because such propositions are not discoverable by experience directly, and if they are inferred from experience, they are unreasonably inferred, unless the falsity of inductive scepticism, which is the very point at issue, is taken for granted. But if, on the other hand, the critic proposes to employ *non*-factual, analytic propositions, as the premisses of his argument against Hume's inductive scepticism, he finds no better reception, for he is now given to understand that such materials are hopelessly unequal to the task which he wishes them to perform.

The critic of Hume incurs special opprobrium, mixed with condescension, if he proposes to draw those non-factual premisses from the theory of logical probability in particular. For then he has merely added one more to 'those numberless critics of [Hume's] ideas who have in the realm of probabilities found an escape from the "scepticism" which he taught'.[1] As one of this host of the damned, who failed to give 'the highest possible credit to the philosophical genius of Hume', the critic of Hume even suffers

[1] This and the following quotation are from G. H. von Wright, *The Logical Problem of Induction* (2nd revised edn.), p. 153.

the ultimate mortification of finding himself allied with a mere statesman![2]

This one-sided attitude to critics of Hume's inductive scepticism, and the absurd interpretation of Hume on which it necessarily rests, were well illustrated by the reception which was accorded by reviewers to D. C. Williams's *The Ground of Induction* around the middle of this century. A less dispersed example is desirable, however, and Popper furnishes one which is as clear as could be wished.

We saw in Chapter 5 section (i) that there is a certain proposition, the truth of which Popper regards as established by 'Hume's criticism of induction' (as well as by his own), and which is simply a special case of what I have identified as being Hume's inductive scepticism (8). This is the statement of logical probability $P(Fa, Fb.t) = P(Fa, t)$.

Now Popper tells us, concerning this comparative equality, that 'every other assumption'—and hence, for example, the natural assessment expressed in the contrary $P(Fa, Fb.t) > P(Fa, t)$— 'would amount to . . . postulating that there is something like a causal connection'[3] between individuals. To assert that Hume's conclusion is false, in other words, would be to assert a certain 'non-logical, a synthetic' proposition, of the nature of a 'natural law'.[4]

Yet it should be evident that, on the contrary, the inequality, $P(Fa, Fb.t) > P(Fa, t)$, is actually a proposition of the same kind as the contrary Humean equality $P(Fa, Fb.t) = P(Fa, t)$. *Both are simply statements of logical probability.* Nor is there any way in which the comparative equality could be proved to be true, distinct from the (ultimately intuitive) way in which the contrary inequality could be proved to be true. In short, the difference between '=' and '>', which is the only difference between the above two statements, cannot mark a difference between a non-factual and a factual proposition. What Popper ought to hold, therefore, in order to be consistent with the remarks quoted above, is that the great inductive sceptic established—that is, that Hume's inductive scepticism itself *is*—an immense factual generalization!

This, however, besides having the effect, which is felt to be intolerable, of placing Hume's thesis on a par with those of his

---

[2] Jan Masaryk, author of *David Hume's Skepsis und die Wahrscheinlichkeitsrechnung.* See on von Wright, op. cit., p. 220 n. 1.

[3] *The Logic of Scientific Discovery* (London, 1959), p. 367. (Here 'casual' is an obvious misprint for 'causal'.) The next phrase quoted is from p. 368.

[4] K. R. Popper, *Conjectures and Refutations* (London, 1963), p. 290.

critics, would be too obvious an absurdity to be enunciated distinctly. The only alternative is therefore to adopt the lesser absurdity, and the one-sided attitude to Hume's critics, which were described above. Accordingly Hume's inductive scepticism is recognized by Popper as being a statement of logical probability, but its denial, on the other hand, although it too is a statement of logical probability, must perforce be represented as being a temerarious assertion about the nature of the actual universe! Hume's '$P(Fa, Fb.t) = P(Fa, t)$' is represented as derivable, and as actually derived by Hume (as indeed it was), from premisses purely *a priori*. But its falsity, on the other hand, is represented as being a proposition of a kind which mere statements of logical probability certainly are utterly incapable of proving.

It should be clear that we are dealing here with an expression of that over-estimation, almost apotheosis, of Hume, which has taken place in the present century, and of which some other expressions are collected below in the Appendix section (*iii*). To correct that over-estimation, and to set in its proper light the corresponding condescension towards Hume's critics which was illustrated above from von Wright, there is just one fact which it is sufficient, but also necessary, to remember. This is, that it is 'in the realm of probabilities' and nowhere else, that Hume's inductive scepticism, no less than what its critics advance, itself belongs.

It will hardly require emphasis that this book does not pretend to make any contribution to the theory of logical probability. On the contrary, the fragments of that theory which I have made use of are so few, and so elementary, that they are certain to appear derisory to the working 'inductive logician' in the Carnapian sense. I am content that they should appear so, since they are so.

In order, however, to prevent a misapprehension of the opposite kind, about what is attempted in the preceding pages, it may be necessary here to emphasize, to the majority of philosophers who are not inductive logicians, a point which was made at length in Chapter 1 section (*v*). For most contemporary philosophers are perhaps likely to feel that even such little technical apparatus as I have employed is necessarily out of place in considering philosophical questions, or at any rate in criticizing a philosopher of the eighteenth century. But the theory of logical probability, if what I have said in Chapter 1 section (*v*) is true, is not what it may appear to be, a branch of non-standard logic which is the business of no one outside a handful of twentieth-century adepts. It is the theory of the degree of conclusiveness of arguments, and assessment of the degree of conclusiveness of arguments is a prominent part of the business of all philosophers at any time. What Hume, in particular, wrote about inductive inference cannot be considered exempt from criticisms aimed at it from the point of view of 'inductive logic' in the Carnapian sense. For despite its lack of technical trappings, Hume's philosophy of induction is not less, though it is not more either, than a rival system of 'inductive logic' to Carnap's. I have merely tried to show, without going outside the range of arguments by which such competing systems must be evaluated, that the verdict in this case must be in favour of Carnap.

There is a feeling which is fairly widespread among philosophers, and certainly more widely current than outright acceptance of Hume's inductive scepticism, that that thesis is some philosophical essence so refined as to be irrefutable, and that even to try to refute it is a mark of bad taste in philosophy. This feeling can subsist only so long as one stays at a safe distance from the text of Hume, and leaves the nature and content of his sceptical thesis correspondingly indefinite. But such an over-readiness to credit inductive scepticism with irrefutability is something which we ought perhaps to expect, on general psychological grounds, after science, and intellectual culture generally, have suffered so deep a shock as they did near the beginning of this century. In such circumstances, as I have said in Chapter 8, inductive fallibilism, at the least, is bound to be embraced. But to some minds, the irrefutability, even if not the truth, of inductive scepticism will suggest itself as being a still better insurance against any repetition of such a shock. Much of the philosophy of science of the present century, indeed, appears to be psychologically intelligible only from this point of view; just as much of the philosophy of science of the preceding century is psychologically intelligible only in the light of the Newtonian *over*-confidence then prevailing.

It may be useful, finally, to draw attention again to the limitedness of what is aimed at in the critical part of this book. I have not attempted to justify induction, or (what perhaps would be the same thing) to refute every possible inductive scepticism. I have attempted to refute just Hume's inductive scepticism, and one of the premisses on which his sole argument for it rests.

APPENDIX

(i) Other arguments in Hume closely related to the argument diagrammed in Chapter 2 above

In this book the only part of Hume's philosophy with which we are concerned is his attack on inductive inference. This attack, we know, takes the form of an argument for a sceptical conclusion concerning one particular kind of induction, viz. predictive-inductive inference. And Hume repeats this argument a number of times.

In reading Hume on 'the understanding', however, one is reminded of the argument about the predictive-inductive inference far more often than is accounted for by actual repetitions of it on Hume's part. There are frequent 'echoes' of the content, and even of the structure, of that argument. There must then be in Hume other arguments, which are rather closely related to his argument about the predictive-inductive inference, and which are the sources of these echoes of it. What are they?

The main one is the argument of the section 'Of the idea of necessary connexion' (*Treatise* Book I Part III section xiv, *Enquiry* section vii).

In both books this section follows the discussion of inductive inference, and Hume's argument about the origin of the idea of necessary connection is in fact a kind of ontological version of his earlier argument about the predictive-inductive inference. Thus it is obvious, I suggest, that Hume's failure to find an 'impression' of necessary connection corresponds, in some sense, to his discovery of the incurable invalidity of the predictive-inductive inference. And stage 1 and stage 2 of Hume's argument about the predictive-inductive inference correspond to his regularly seeking that elusive 'impression', first in a single instance of the conjunction of two observable properties, and then in 'several instances'.

To explain clearly and fully what the connections are between Hume's argument about the predictive-inductive inference and his argument about necessary connection, as distinct from perceiving more or less distinctly that such connections exist, would not be very easy; and it would hardly be even possible without entering deeply into the subject of causation. Fortunately it is not necessary for me to attempt such an explanation. Hume's argument about the predictive-inductive inference (and by implication his attack on inductive inference in general) is so clear and self-contained that it can perfectly well be considered on its own, as it has been considered in this book.

The other source of echoes of the argument about the predictive-inductive inference is this. As soon as he has advanced that argument, Hume immediately propounds, both in the *Treatise* and the *Enquiry*, a certain minor variant of it. The original argument concerns, of course, conjunctions of two observable properties (such as flame and heat). The variant concerns conjunctions of an observable property with the *power* (sufficient) to produce a certain other observable property. With this variation the argument proceeds, through stage 1 and stage 2, just as before.

This variant of the argument about the predictive-inductive inference will be found in the *Treatise* from p. 90 (the middle of the second paragraph) to p. 92 (at top); and in the *Enquiry* from p. 36 (near foot) to p. 38 (end of first paragraph). There is even a micro-version of it (too short, however, to have any internal structure, or even for its purpose to be clear if we did not have the other, longer versions to help us) in the *Abstract*: at p. 294, second paragraph, the last two sentences.

'Power' being akin to 'necessary connexion', the two arguments mentioned above are of course connected not only with the argument about the predictive-inductive inference but also with each other.

(ii) Treatise *Book I Part III sections xi–xiii*

These are the sections 'Of the probability of chances', 'Of the probability of causes', and 'Of unphilosophical probability'. In the text of the present book these sections, or at any rate everything that is peculiar to them, have been totally neglected. They are discussed here in order to show that, in a book with the subject of the present one, that neglect is (despite what the titles of these sections might lead one to expect) altogether justified.

The 'probability' with which this book is concerned is, of course, the logical probability which is to be ascribed to what Hume calls 'probability'; that is, to what he calls 'probable arguments'; that is (if what was said in Chapter 2 above was correct) to inductive inferences. For it is to be remembered: that the whole of Book I Part III of the *Treatise* is entitled 'Of knowledge and probability'; that all of that Part (except section i, 'Of knowledge') is about 'probability', in Hume's (wide) sense of that word; and that what it is in fact about (except for sections xi–xiii) is the degree of conclusiveness of a typical inductive inference, viz. the predictive-inductive inference; along with a topic which (see the preceding section of this Appendix) is closely related specifically to that kind of inductive inference.

What sections xi–xiii are about, Hume announces (as we saw in the text) at the beginning of xi. They are about 'some other species of reasoning' (p. 124), other, that is, than the predictive-inductive inference. Of these 'other species' the most important for Hume, he makes quite clear (p. 130), is the inductive inference to an unobserved instance from the 'frequent', as contrasted with the 'constant conjunction' (p. 139) of two observable properties. (The class of inferences, that is, of which our paradigm was: 'Nearly all of the many ships observed leaving port in the past have returned safely, and this is a ship leaving port, so, this will return safely.') This kind of inference is the main subject of section xii. The subjects of sections xi and xiii are other kinds of inference again; and still other kinds are very briefly discussed at the end of xii, p. 142. The differentia, however, of all of the kinds of inference which were to be discussed in sections xi–xiii was this: that unlike the predictive-inductive inference, they are all 'attended with uncertainty' (p. 124). For as we saw in the text, Hume begins section xi by clearly announcing a change in his application of the word 'probability'. Up to this point (and consequently, in those sections which occupied us in the text of this book), he had used that word, he says, 'to comprehend *all* our arguments from causes or effects' (p. 124, my italics), *all* 'arguments from experience' (*Enquiry*, p. 56 n.). Now, however (that is, in sections xi–xiii), he proposes to give it a narrower application, by confining it to just such of the former class of inferences as are 'attended with uncertainty'.

As to what was Hume's purpose in discussing these other kinds of inference, it will suffice to quote again the opening paragraph of section xi. 'But in order to bestow on this system its full force and evidence, we must carry our eye from it a moment to consider its consequences, and explain from the same principles some other species of reasoning, which are derived from the same origin.' (p. 124.) Hume's purpose, then, was to illustrate and confirm, by reference to other kinds of inference (mainly the inference from frequent conjunction), 'principles' which he has enunciated distinctly at length already; viz. in connection with the predictive-inductive inference. But this means that sections xi–xiii are not central to Hume's philosophy of inductive inference. The essence of that philosophy has been given in his account, now completed, of the one kind of inductive inference which is 'entirely free from doubt and uncertainty' (p. 124), and the treatment of which by Hume occupied us to the exclusion of all others in the text of the present book.

This estimate of sections xi–xiii, as an inessential part of Hume's philosophy of inductive inference, is quite certainly one which was shared by Hume himself. In the *Abstract*, '... wherein the chief argument of [the *Treatise*] is further Illustrated and Explained', Hume's subject is of course the predictive-inductive inference (and the related idea of necessary connection); the materials of sections xi–xiii, on the other hand, are nowhere to be seen. In the *Enquiry* the thirty full pages which these sections occupy in the *Treatise* shrink to the mere three pages which make up section vi of that book. And it would not be easy to say in what way the *Enquiry* would have been the worse, if those three pages had been omitted altogether.

But sections xi–xiii are not only an inessential part of Hume's philosophy of induction. They are, philosophically considered, altogether unrewarding intrinsically. Commentators on Hume have without exception failed to extract from them anything of philosophical interest. Their best aids, in dealing with these sections, have been brevity or even silence, and mere paraphrase or (still more non-committal) quotation. And there are ample reasons for this state of affairs.

The most important single reason is that, in sections xi–xiii, the kind of interest which Hume displays, in the inferences he is discussing, is an empirical, psychological interest, rather than a logico-philosophical and evaluative one. The philosophical passages in these sections seem to me, indeed, to be confined to two short ones: pp. 126–7 and pp. 139–40. And even the first of these is abruptly broken off by Hume saying 'the question is . . .'—a certain factual one. There was, of course (though we were not concerned with it), a psychological side to Hume's discussion of the predictive-inductive inference, too; but it did not there blot out the philosophical side of his subject. In sections xi–xiii it does.

Another reason, almost equally important, for the difficulties which commentators have encountered in dealing with sections xi–xiii is their downright obscurity. This applies to the little philosophy that these sections do contain, but it applies no less to the would-be psychology of which they chiefly consist. I at any rate have not been able to understand Hume's detailed account of the psychology of the inference about the ships (in xii), or of the inference about the die (in xi).

As an illustration of the obstacles which lie in the way of such understanding, the following sentence will serve. Hume writes, in connection with the die, that 'the original impulse, and consequently the vivacity of thought, arising from the causes, is divided and split in pieces by the intermingled chances' (p. 129). Nor does the context in which this is said do more than render it a little less obscure than it would be on its own.

The same sentence will serve also to illustrate the fact that very often in sections xi–xiii even Hume's *language* is curiously embarrassed. Sometimes, for example, as here, his use of the word 'chances' is like no other that ever was on land or sea. There is nothing which clearly oversteps the bounds of intelligible English in speaking of an 'impulse', or 'the vivacity of thought', as being 'split in pieces' by something or other; but to speak of this as being done 'by the . . . *chances*' clearly does. And to speak as Hume does of 'a mixture of causes *among the chances*' (p. 126), or of 'intermingled *chances*' (intermingled, presumably, again among 'the causes'), is little or no better.

Appendix

It would be very easy to multiply examples of perplexed English in sections xi–xiii, but one more short example must suffice. On p. 124, having just introduced his narrowed sense of 'probability' which confines it to inductive inferences attended with uncertainty, Hume begins a new paragraph thus: 'Probability, or reasoning from conjecture . . .' Now, given the context just referred to, the supposition is unavoidable that Hume has managed to say here the precise opposite of what he meant; that is, that he meant reasoning not 'from' but '*to*' a conjecture. And if so he has made the most unpromising beginning imaginable for a discussion of *inferences*.

Hume himself was well aware, at least by the time he reached the midpoint of these three sections, that he was making extremely heavy weather of it all. He admits (p. 135) the 'air of subtilty which attends' his psychological explanation of the inference from frequent conjunction, and again, in the same connection, confesses himself 'sensible how abstruse all this reasoning must appear to the generality of readers' (p. 138). In between the last two quoted passages he almost desperately makes a fresh start: 'Here is almost the same argument in a different light' (p. 137). And on p. 139 he is actually back at his very starting point. For he here recapitulates the two 'principles which we have found to be sufficiently convincing even with regard to our most certain reasonings from causation' (i.e. the conclusions (d) and (j) in our diagram of the argument about the predictive-inductive inference), and then says of them: 'But I shall venture to affirm, that with regard to these conjectural or probable reasonings [i.e. the subject-matter of sections xi–xiii] they still acquire a new degree of evidence.' That is precisely what, in the very first paragraph of these three sections, Hume had undertaken to establish. Yet it is also what, fifteen pages later, he recognizes he must still 'venture to affirm'!

Sometimes, in these sections, indeed, the clouds do part. But the result is not always to light up something of value. For example, Hume's psychological account of the 'ship' inference leads him to affirm, in all seriousness, that 'a man, who desires a thousand pound, has in reality a thousand or more desires . . .' (p. 141). This proposition is certainly a *reductio ad absurdum* of something in Hume's premisses; but it must be doubted whether it would be philosophically rewarding to try to find out what.

There is, as the reader may have noticed, one passage from these sections of which I have made use in the text above (Chapter 2). This is the italicized pair of sentences from p. 139. But of course these are simply that recapitulation, referred to in the last paragraph but one, of the conclusions (d) and (j) of the two stages of Hume's earlier argument which is the subject of this book; except that, in order to comprehend the kind of inference under discussion in section xii, (j) now says that 'even after the *frequent or* constant conjunction' of observable properties, 'we have no reason', etc.

We have now seen some of the difficulties which lie in the way of philosophical consideration of sections xi–xiii. I propose next to set down briefly whatever in those sections seems to me to be, in spite of the difficulties, both clear, and of at any rate *potential* philosophical interest.

First, the general topic of the three sections is clear. It is those species of the genus, 'inductive inferences', which are 'attended with uncertainty'; or in different words, which no one mistakes for valid inferences.

Second, the topic of section xii is clear. It is that particular species, among inductive inferences attended with uncertainty, of which the inference about the ships is a paradigm; in other words, the inductive inference to a new instance from the frequent but not constant conjunction of two observable properties.

Third, the topic of section xi is—I believe, but here one must be more tentative—the Bernoullian inference to a singular conclusion, of which the following may serve as a paradigm: 'This is a fair die marked in the usual way, and it is about to be thrown, so, this throw will not result in a "four".' (The major premiss here may alternatively be phrased as, 'The chance', or again 'The factual probability', 'of throwing "four" with this die $= \frac{1}{6}$.')

One of the reasons why this suggestion must be made with some tentativeness is that it is inconsistent with the view taken above of what the general topic of xi–xiii is. If I was right in arguing, in the text, that 'probable arguments' in Hume's wide sense are simply inductive arguments, then, since his sense of 'probability' in xi–xiii is quite certainly just a narrower sense than his earlier one, the arguments considered in xi–xiii, whatever their differentia, must still belong to the genus 'inductive arguments'. They must still be, consequently, 'arguments from experience'; that is, their premisses would have to be observational. But the above Bernoullian inference is not inductive, since one of its premisses is not observational. An assessment of the chance (or factual probability) of throwing 'four' with a certain die, is not an observation-statement.

The same difficulty may arise with at least one of the kinds of inference under discussion in section xiii. At least, if what Hume calls reasoning 'from general rules' (pp. 146 ff.) is what that name suggests, it too would not be a kind of argument from experience, since its premisses would not be observational.

I do not know how to resolve this inconsistency. But it would be an utterly insufficient ground for rejecting my thesis that, in the sections which concerned us in the text of this book, Hume meant by 'probable arguments', inductive arguments. For (to mention only one reason) it is possible that the topic of section xi is *not* the above Bernoullian inference. Hume may instead have had in mind the inference, to the next throw of a die, from the observed relative frequency of 'four' with that die. This is really a totally different kind of inference, of course, and the topic of xi, if this were it, would reduce to the topic of xii, since *this* inference about the die is just the 'ship' inference over again. But, it is interesting to notice, Hume does appear to suggest in the first paragraph of xii that (because 'chance' is unreal) the inference discussed in xi *does* somehow reduce to that discussed in xii. And the topic of xi, on this interpretation of it, really would be an inductive inference.

The topic of xi having been at least tentatively identified, the next question is, what are the kinds of inference which are the topic of the remaining section, xiii? But to this I am unable to return any answer definite enough to be worth setting down. Section xiii defies any treatment other than silence, paraphrase, or quotation.

One thing is clear, however, about the kinds of inferences discussed in xiii. This is that they are inferences which it is usual to regard as 'unphilosophical'; that is, as unscientific or unreasonable. For Hume begins xiii by contrasting the subject-matter of it with the inferences he has just discussed in xi and xii. Referring back to the inductive inference about the ships, and (on my interpretation of xi) to the Bernoullian inference about the die, he writes (p. 143): 'All these kinds of probability are receiv'd by philosophers, and allow'd to be reasonable foundations of belief and opinion. But there are others, that are deriv'd from the same principles, tho' they have not had the good fortune to obtain the same sanction.'

We now have clearly in mind the kinds of inference which are the topics of at least some of these sections. We are, surely, entitled to assume that Hume's interest in these inferences was, at least partly, evaluative. We may, therefore, properly ask: what were some of the evaluative conclusions which Hume reached on these topics? The answer must be that in sections xi–xiii there is nothing which one can point to as being an evaluative conclusion of Hume concerning even one of the kinds of inference under discussion there. It was not so, of course, in the earlier sections, concerning the predictive-inductive inference; there Hume's evaluative conclusion (viz. scepticism) stood out perfectly plainly. But here Hume is far too absorbed in displaying the ability of his 'system' to explain various empirical psychological 'phenomena' (p. 154), to draw any evaluative conclusion at all, sceptical or otherwise.

What Hume's assessment *was*, of the degree of conclusiveness of the inferences here discussed, is nevertheless perfectly clear of course. It is the same as his assessment of the predictive-inductive inference: that is, it is a sceptical one. For, for one thing, it will hardly be suggested that Hume regarded the inductive inference from mere frequent conjunction, for example, as being more conclusive than that from constant conjunction.

Again, although the natural assessments of the former inference, and of the Bernoullian inference about the die, are of course favourable, Hume makes it quite clear that he does not share that assessment. Inferences of those two kinds are, as he says (p. 143), 'receiv'd by philosophers, and allowed to be reasonable foundations of belief and opinion'; and it is not only by philosophers, of course, that they are so 'receiv'd'. The unreasonable inferences discussed in section xiii, Hume says, although 'deriv'd from the same principles', simply 'have not had *the good fortune* to obtain the same' favourable assessment (p. 143, my italics). Clearly Hume does not believe that between, say, the inference about the ships, and certain 'unphilosophical' inferences, there is a real as distinct from a supposed difference in degree of conclusiveness.

Granted that Hume's assessments of the inferences discussed in xi and xii are sceptical ones, does he *argue* for these assessments here, and if so how? Hume says, concerning the Bernoullian inference about the die, that 'here we may repeat all the same arguments' (p. 126) which he had employed concerning the predictive-inductive inference; and, at the middle of p. 139, he appears to say the same concerning the inductive inference about the ships. At both of these places, in fact, he intimates that he is actually about to repeat that argument, presumably *mutatis mutandis*. But he does not do so. What he immediately goes on to say is, indeed, a recognizable variant of stage 1 of his argument about the predictive-inductive inference. But in the next paragraph in each of these places (viz. the top half of p. 127, and the last paragraph begun on p. 139), where one would therefore expect an adaptation of stage 2 of that argument, there is no recognizable variant of stage 2. What the argument of either of these paragraphs *is*, I am unable to say.

Hume could hardly be said, then, even to have seriously tried to argue for a sceptical assessment of the inferences which he discussed in sections xi and xii. If he had seriously tried to adapt stage 2 of his earlier argument to them, he would have encountered formidable difficulties. But it would take us much too far afield if we were to begin now to explore how Hume *might* have argued in order to extend his scepticism to those 'other species of reasoning'.

Of the actual contents of sections xi-xiii, everything which seems to me both clear and of even potential philosophical interest has now been reported. It will be evident that, unless my report has been grossly deficient, the neglect of those sections in the text of this book was justified. They are so extraordinarily unrewarding, indeed, that some special explanation of the fact seems called for. Such an explanation is not far to seek, if certain things which are said in the text of this book are true.

The fallibilist thesis, it was there said, is an important truth, at least in connection with the predictive-inductive inference. It is so, because the natural assessment of that inference, at least at the 'organic' level, is not only favourable but even mistakes the predictive-inductive inference for a valid one. This psychological fact gives the fallibilist thesis something to correct, and imparts even to the sceptical assessment of that inference the merit of avoiding a deeply natural error. In connection with the predictive-inductive inference, too, the assumption of deductivism escapes immediate recognition as a short and sure step to an incredible (sceptical) conclusion, and it does so for the same reason: that the fallibility of the predictive-inductive inference (which is the other premiss needed for the sceptical conclusion) is not genuinely obvious to us.

The case is entirely the opposite, however, with the inductive inference from frequent conjunction, and with the Bernoullian inference about the die. These are inferences 'attended with uncertainty': inferences, that is to say, of which the natural assessment, while favourable of course, is not at all such as to mistake them for valid inferences. To assert the fallibility of these inferences would be to assert no more than is, to everyone, totally obvious. Again, to assume the deductivist thesis in connection with these inferences would be self-discrediting, as being a transparent veil for scepticism, and again for the same reason: that the fallibility of these inferences (which is the other premiss needed for a sceptical conclusion) *is* genuinely obvious to us.

Contrapositively, then, a man who did assume deductivism, as Hume did, could hardly take a serious evaluative interest in the kinds of inference which are the subject of sections xi–xiii. The predictive-inductive inference is the only inductive inference which pretends to the only high degree of conclusiveness which a deductivist recognizes. And *that* pretension Hume has already successfully punctured. How could he take seriously the claims to a high degree of conclusiveness of other inferences which do not even pretend to be valid? Such a man could hardly take, in such inferences, any kind of interest other than an empirical and psychological one.

(iii) Some examples of twentieth-century exaggeration of Hume's achievement

Hume has acquired in the present century a reputation far higher than he ever enjoyed before; and at least in connection with inductive inference, if what has been said in this book is true, a reputation even higher than he deserves. To show that this is true, it will suffice to collect some instances in which twentieth-century writers claim to have found in Hume's writings on induction some thesis or argument, which had not been found there before, and which in fact is not there. This is what is done below.

What a writer erroneously attributes to Hume is usually something of which the writer himself strongly approves: as is natural enough in the present century (though in the nineteenth century the temptation was of a precisely opposite nature). But some of these attributions bear so little relation to the text on which they are based as to recall Lewis Carroll's character who

> ... thought he saw an Argument
> That proved he was the Pope:
> He looked again, and found it was
> A Bar of Mottled Soap.

(a) Chapter VII of Keynes's *Treatise on Probability* is a 'Historical Retrospect', and on pp. 81–3 there is a discussion of the classical theory of probability. Keynes points out that the classical theorists relied heavily, for the assessment of probabilities, on the 'Principle of Indifference' which he has in an earlier chapter criticized severely. This reliance, Keynes has shown, was one of the sources of the extravagant claims made for the theory of probability by Laplace and other French writers of 'the latter half of the eighteenth century' (p. 83 n. 1).

Yet [Keynes goes on] the new principles did not win acceptance without opposition. D'Alembert, Hume and Ancillon stand out as the sceptical critics of probability, against the credulity of eighteenth-century philosophers, who were ready to swallow without too many questions the conclusions of a science which claimed and seemed to bring an entire new field within the dominion of Reason.

The first effective criticism came from Hume, who was also the first to distinguish the method of Locke and the philosophers from the method of Bernoulli and the mathematicians. 'Probability', he says, 'or reasoning from conjecture, may be divided into two kinds, *viz.*, that which is founded on *chance* and that which arises from causes'. By these two kinds he evidently means the mathematical method of counting the equal chances based on Indifference, and the inductive method based on the experience of uniformity. He argues that 'chance' alone can be the foundation of nothing, and 'that there must always be a mixture of causes among the chances, in order to be the foundation of any reasoning'. His previous argument against probabilities, which were based on an assumption of cause, is thus extended to the mathematical method also (p. 83).

Both of the quotations from Hume in this passage are from the early paragraphs of section xi of Book I Part III of the *Treatise*, and it is evidently in that part of the Hume corpus that Keynes finds 'effective criticism' of the classical theory of probability. But what does this passage of Keynes say?

Hume's scepticism, as we have seen in the preceding section of this Appendix, undoubtedly did extend to the 'other species of reasoning' which he discussed in sections xi and xii. As for justification of extending his scepticism to them, however, we have seen that Hume could scarcely be said even to have tried to supply any. Yet Keynes (in the last sentence of the above passage) represents this extension as a successfully established conclusion. As to *how* Hume had adapted his argument for scepticism to these other kinds of inference, Keynes does not venture words of his own. He prefers direct quotation from Hume, even when it means quoting a sentence which is not only obscure, but scarcely intelligible English—that 'there must always be a mixture of causes among the chances', etc. How this thesis, if it can be called that, accomplishes the extension in question, Keynes seems to think obvious; whereas it could hardly be less so.

And precisely *what* was the criticism ('effective', at that) which Hume made, whether of the classical theory in general or the Principle of Indifference in particular, Keynes leaves equally unclear. It is impossible to discover from the above passage what it was. Yet it is from this very passage that it must be elicited, if it is to be discovered at all. For Keynes never again refers to this mythical 'criticism', and no other writer has lent his name to this particular claim on Hume's behalf.

It ought not to be overlooked that what Keynes's 'Historical Retrospect' implies, about Hume's relation to the classical theory in the second half of the eighteenth century, is anachronistic on its very face. Laplace was not even born until ten years after Book I of the *Treatise* was published. And at the time when Hume was writing that book, Bernoulli's *Ars Conjectandi*, which is the earliest work from which the classical theory can possibly be dated, and which is itself relatively free from the pretensions which were later rested partly on it, had been before the world a bare twenty years.

(b) This example also concerns section xi of Book I Part III of the *Treatise*.

In a 1962 (Fontana Library) edition of Book I, the editor, Professor D. G. C. Macnabb, has appended a footnote to the end of the eighth paragraph. It reads: 'Up to this point the section is a masterly non-technical introduction to the calculus of chances.'

This claim is unlike all the others collected in the present section, in that even if it were true, the fact would not be of any importance for the philosophy of induction or of probability. Hume certainly could have written an introduction to the calculus of chances, and it is of historical interest only whether in fact he did so.

But as an example of twentieth-century historiography *ad maiorem gloriam* of Hume, the above footnote is remarkable, even breathtaking. There is no 'introduction to the calculus of chances' in the first eight paragraphs of section xi—neither a 'masterly non-technical' one, nor any other. 'And this' (as Hume wrote in another connection)[1] 'is a matter of fact which is easily cleared and ascertained.'

---

[1] *My Own Life*, the last sentence.

(c) Wherever Hume's attack on inductive inference has been admitted to be at least partly successful, the most common reaction to it has always been one which could be expressed as follows. 'True, no inductive inferences can ever attain the highest possible degree of conclusiveness; but some of them are of high logical probability nevertheless.' For as we have seen in Chapter 8, the historical effect of Hume's argument against induction has on the whole been to secure the acceptance of inductive fallibilism, while failing to secure the acceptance of inductive scepticism; and the first and second clauses above respectively reflect these historical facts. This reaction to Hume is not only the common one, but, just because of the almost-universal acceptance of inductive fallibilism, has come to sound, to our ears, distinctly banal. Accordingly I shall refer to it as 'the commonplace reaction' to Hume's attack on inductive inference.

If what I have said in the text of this book is true, the commonplace reaction to Hume is also the correct one. Not, of course, that I tried to prove the truth of its second clause (only the falsity of the sceptical contrary of it). But if what I have said is true, the first clause concedes all that is proved by the true premisses of Hume's argument; the first and second clauses together require the rejection of Hume's implicit deductivism; and once deductivism is rejected there is no longer anything in Hume's premisses which would prevent us from making the natural favourable assessment of some inductive inferences—which is what the second clause does.

Now, the common reaction to Hume's argument could not have been the one stated above, if it had been believed that one of the *targets* of Hume's attack was the thesis that some inductive inferences, although invalid, are nevertheless of a high degree of conclusiveness. For this thesis is the commonplace reaction to Hume's argument (or what is essential in it). It is precisely what most thinkers have believed that they could still claim for inductive inference, even after conceding to Hume everything (viz. inductive fallibilism) which could no longer be denied him. Clearly, then, it has usually been believed, at any rate, that Hume did not have, as one of the targets of his attack, the thesis that some inductive inferences are of high logical probability although invalid.

By the middle of the twentieth century, however, a reaction had begun against the commonplace reaction to Hume. This was to be expected, as inductive fallibilism became a complete commonplace, and even began to be made into a truism, while at the same time Hume's reputation was rising to an unprecedented height. Under these circumstances, the thought was almost bound to suggest itself, that the commonplace reaction did insufficient justice to the profundity of Hume's argument against induction. An evasive stratagem which is now so easy (it would then be thought), must surely have been anticipated, and defeated, by Hume himself. Accordingly, it began to be claimed that Hume had in fact forestalled, and *a fortiori* that he *had* had as one of the objects of his attack, the thesis that some inductive arguments have a high though not the highest possible degree of conclusiveness.

The following are some expressions of this novel claim.

Some have tried to save the situation by admitting that all scientific inference is probable inference. But Hume's sceptical attack applies with equal force to probable inference.[2]

Can we not, however, argue that while experience yields no *certainty* as to the future, it may yet instruct us as to what is *likely* to happen in the future? But this, too, as Hume points out, is 'no thoroughfare'.[3]

In other words Hume points out that we get involved in an infinite regress if we appeal to experience in order to justify *any* conclusion concerning unobserved instances—*even mere probable conclusions*, as he adds in his *Abstract* (p. 15).[4]

It deserves mention that David Hume, who was the first to see that general synthetical propositions cannot be proved *a priori*, also clearly apprehended that this result of the impossibility of foretelling the future cannot be 'evaded' or 'minimised' by reference to probability.[5]

It will be evident to the reader that if what I have said in the text of this book is true, then what these authors imply must be false. A man could not possibly have been intending to refute the thesis that some inductive inferences are of a high degree of conclusiveness *though invalid*, if throughout his argument he simply *assumed* that invalidity suffices to make an inference (whether inductive or of any other kind) unreasonable. The evidence, therefore, for thinking that the authors quoted above are mistaken, is the evidence for thinking that Hume took for granted the truth of deductivism.

That evidence I have given as well as I can in the text, where I tried to show that deductivism enters Hume's argument as a suppressed premiss not just once but twice. (See Chapter 3 section (*iii*).) And in this respect (as was also remarked in the text), my detailed account of Hume's argument has on its side the opinion, vague but overwhelmingly preponderant among writers on Hume, that Hume's conception of 'reason', or of an inference which reason can sanction, was an exclusively 'rationalistic' or 'deductive' one.

For substantiation of their claim quoted above, Popper and von Wright both refer to the *Abstract*, p. 15 in the original pagination which was

[2] A. H. Basson, *David Hume* (London, 1958), pp. 167–8.
[3] N. Kemp Smith, *The Philosophy of David Hume* (London, 1960), pp. 374–5.
[4] K. Popper, *The Logic of Scientific Discovery* (London, 1959), p. 369. Cf. ibid. p. 265, starred addition to n. 2. And cf. the same author's *Conjectures and Refutations* (London, 1963), pp. 192–3, 289.
[5] G. H. von Wright, *The Logical Problem of Induction* (London, 1957), p. 153. Cf. ibid. p. 176.

reproduced in the edition by Keynes and Sraffa; that is, to a passage which, in the edition by Flew, begins on the sixth-last line of p. 293 and ends with the first paragraph of p. 294. And this reference furnishes a clue as to how the above mistaken claim for Hume may have originated. For that passage, far from being what Popper says it was, one which was *added* in the *Abstract*, turns out to be nothing but the *Abstract* version of stage 2 of Hume's argument, diagrammed in Chapter 2 above, against the predictive-inductive inference. In it, therefore, if the view taken in this book is correct, Hume's phrase 'probable arguments' had the purely non-evaluative sense of 'arguments from experience', 'inductive arguments'.

Our sense of 'probable arguments' on the other hand, as was remarked in the text, is purely evaluative, and in particular it is precisely that which the writers quoted above evidently take to have been Hume's: 'arguments of high degree of conclusiveness though invalid'. In order to have at least a partial explanation, therefore, of the exaggerated claims for Hume which were quoted above, one would need to suppose only that their authors mistook Hume's sense of 'probable arguments' for our sense of that phrase.

The most likely place for such a mistake to have first crept in is at element (i) in stage 2 of Hume's argument. Yet Hume uses the phrase 'probable arguments' at the very outset of stage 2 (in element (e)), where it refers obviously enough to the kind of inferences which were his subject-matter throughout Book I Part III of the *Treatise*, the *Abstract*, and sections iv-vi of the *Enquiry*; which can hardly be supposed to be anything other than inductive inferences. And even the context of element (i) is such as should have made it quite clear that anything inconsistent with deductivism was as far as possible from Hume's mind. For Hume's argument down to (i) and (g) was the result of his asking how one could *prove*[6] a certain proposition which was necessary for the *validity* of certain inductive inferences.

The reaction against the commonplace reaction to Hume in its turn provoked some reaction in the 1960s: first from Professor A. Flew,[7] then from the present writer.[8]

(d) The passage which was quoted in (c) above, in which von Wright claims that Hume's argument cannot be evaded or minimized as it commonly has been, continues as follows:

He [Hume] was aware of the infinite retrogression to which the introduction of probabilities in this connection leads and also of the necessity of interpreting

---

[6] See the passage of the *Abstract*, referred to in the last paragraph but one, on which Popper and von Wright base their claim quoted above. It contains the word 'prove' twice; 'proved' once; and 'proof' four times.
[7] In his *Hume's Philosophy of Belief* (London, 1961), pp. 75-6.
[8] In the *Philosophical Review* for April 1965.

probability as a statistical concept if it is to be of relevance to statements on future events.

To substantiate these two further claims for Hume, von Wright gives two references, one appended to 'infinite retrogression', the second to the end of the above sentence. Let us consider the second claim, and its textual backing, first.

It would not be difficult to show that the supposed 'necessity of interpreting probability as a statistical concept if it is to be of relevance to statements on future events' is illusory.[9] But to do so is not necessary for my present purpose, which is not philosophical but historical. So for the sake of the argument let us concede to von Wright the alleged necessity. The question is, where was it that Hume displayed his prescience with respect to this necessity?

The relevant footnote[10] refers us, yet again, to p. 15 (in the original pagination) of the *Abstract*. But that is (as we have seen in (c) above) just to stage 2 of Hume's argument about the predictive-inductive inference!

Once again, then, at this part of the text Hume's 'probable arguments' meant simply 'inductive arguments', if what has been said in this book is correct; and if so then von Wright's claim must certainly be mistaken. But the best way to deal with this claim is, as we dealt with Macnabb's claim in (b) above, by direct appeal to the relevant texts. I affirm then, that in Hume's argument, about the predictive-inductive inference there is *no* sign of an awareness on his part of a 'necessity of interpreting probability as a statistical concept', etc.; and the reader is invited to satisfy himself of the fact, by re-reading the relevant passages: which are: *Treatises*, pp. 87–90, *Abstract*, pp. 293–4, *Enquiry*, pp. 35–6.

Now as to the first claim made for Hume in the above quotation. This must be false, if what was said in (c) above was true. If Hume did not forestall the commonplace reaction to his argument, then *a fortiori* he did not forestall it by discovering an infinite regress in it.

This claim that if one says that some inductive inferences are of high but not the highest possible degree of conclusiveness, one is led into an infinite regress, is a surprising claim to say the least. But let us, as before, suppose for the sake of the argument that it is true. Our concern is with the still more surprising historical claim, that Hume was aware of this interesting fact (as Carnap, for example, never was). Where was it that, according to von Wright, Hume showed this particular piece of prescience?

The relevant footnote[11] refers us to Book I Part IV section i of the *Treatise*, 'Of scepticism with regard to reason'.

[9] Cf. my review of W. C. Salmon, *The Foundations of Scientific Inference*, in the *Australasian Journal of Philosophy* for May 1969, p. 88.
[10] *The Logical Problem of Induction*, p. 223 n. 16. [11] Op. cit. p. 223 n. 15.

The argument of that section need not be expounded here. It is, and has been generally recognized as being, not merely defective, but one of the worst arguments ever to impose itself on a man of genius. (Hume was not, even so, deceived by it for long: the argument was never repeated after the *Treatise*.) But let us further suppose, for the sake of von Wright's claim for it, that the argument was not defective. What then?

The section is rightly called 'scepticism with regard to *reason*'. For Hume's subject-matter here is not inductive inference, but all kinds of inference indifferently, quite explicitly including valid inference from premisses necessarily true. The 'sceptical' conclusion reached here, therefore (the particular nature of which need not detain us), extends indifferently to all inferences whatever.

It is at least misleading, then, to suggest that the argument of the *Treatise* Book I Part IV section i is an argument against 'the introduction of probabilities *in this connection*': i.e. in connection with inductive inference, the only place where the commonplace reaction to Hume does introduce it.

It is true, however, that the kind of scepticism, whatever it is, which is argued for in that section, would include inductive inference in its scope. But now mark another consequence of endorsing that argument, as von Wright clearly does. The effect of the argument, as we have seen, is to involve all inference in a common ruin. It will thus *inter alia* obliterate a distinction, on which rests the whole of Hume's own argument in Book I Part III for inductive scepticism, and even his argument for inductive fallibilism: *the distinction between valid and invalid inferences*. This is also a distinction which is of considerable importance to other philosophers, including von Wright himself.

But apparently Hume must be praised even though the heavens fall.

INDEX OF NAMES

(*Hume's name appears so frequently that no entry is given for it here*)

Aristotle, 81 n., 94

Bacon, F., 81 n., 95
Basson, A. H., 129 n.
Bayes, T., 101-2
Berkeley, G., 94
Bernoulli, J., 67-8, 101-2
Broad, C. D., 110

Carnap, R., 2, 5-10, 15-16, 18 n., 22-3, 60, 68 n., 75, 92, 104-5, 107, 115-16, 131
Carroll, L., 126
Cox, R. T., 8 n.

de Moivre, A., 100 n.
de Morgan, A., 103 n.

Edwards, P., 107-10
Einstein, A., 104
Euclid, 81 n., 108

Flew, A., 27 n., 107 n., 130
Fowler, T., 99, 103

Galton, F., 103 n.

Hall, R., 51 n.
Herschel, J., 103
Herschel, W., 103 n.

Jeffreys, H., 8 n.
Jevons, W. S., 103-4
Johnson, W. E., 8 n.

Kant, I., 5, 94
Kemp Smith, N., 129
Keynes, J. M., 2, 7, 8, 11, 59, 68, 70, 76 n., 85, 89, 100, 101 n., 111, 126-7, 130

Lacroix, S. F., 102
Lakatos, I., 18 n.
Laplace, 67-8, 79 n., 101-4, 107, 127
Leibniz, G., 94

Mach, E., 103-4
Mackie, J. L., 30 n.
Macnabb, D. G. C., 127, 131
Masaryk, J., 114 n.
Mill, J. S., 81 n., 94-5, 98, 103
Miller, D. S., 51-2 n.
Mossner, E. C., 49, 90

Newton, I., 93-5, 100, 104

Passmore, J. A., 90
Pearson, K., 103
Popper, K. R., 18 n., 65-6, 104, 114-15, 129-30
Price, J. V., 49 n.
Pythagoras, 5

Quetelet, A., 101-3

Ramsey, F. P., 89
Russell, B., 110

Salmon, W. C., 2, 131 n.
Selby-Bigge, L. A., 27 n.
Sraffa, P., 130

Todhunter, I., 101 n.

von Thun, M., 68-73, 87-8, 112-13
von Wright, G. H., 102, 113-15, 129-32

Williams, D. C., 105, 114
Wittgenstein, L., 88, 104